BLAGDON LOC.. HISTORY SOCIETY

A History of Blagdon

VOLUME 3

to be published as a series of journals

The Prodigal Son
C15th misericord from St Andrew's Parish Church, Blagdon

November 2007

Editor - Neil Bentham

Assistant Editors - Peter King & Sheila Johnson

Cover Photograph: Postcard c1910 Blagdon High Street from The George Symes Collection, (BLHS Archive). Clockwise from left: Blacksmith Humphries, The George Inn, BLHS HQ (now known as Court Lodge) and W.J. Taylor Supply Stores.

Typeset in Bembo
Imprint: GWP / FWB. England
Funded by a grant from the Local Heritage Initiative

Local Heritage *initiative*

ISBN 978-0-9548125-5-3

Contents

Introduction

This is the third volume of a history of our village and it will be evident to the reader that, as the depth of the research into the various topics increases and more information is unearthed, so the volumes are becoming gradually more weighty. In fact, such is the length of some of the articles, it became obvious that what was to be Volume 3 would have to be reduced to a more manageable size and therefore Volume 4 was created alongside it. Both volumes are being printed in 2007, with Volume 3 becoming available in December, when the Editor hopes that a few copies might turn up in sundry Christmas stockings, and volume 4 being available in February 2008 to mark the tenth anniversary of the founding of the Society.

All credit is due to the authors for their efforts, and it is hoped that both the members of the Society and the wider community may find something of interest and perhaps illumination in various aspects of Blagdon's past.

As an adjunct to the published histories, 9th August 2007 saw the launch of a unique oral record of recollections and observations on life in this Mendip village, by locals who lived here and personalities from slightly further afield who contributed so much and had an interest in the village. Tony Staveacre assiduously recorded over thirty years the voices of the people, and with the assistance of Allen Harris, Pete Hicks, John Cluett, David Mayo and Julie Chamberlain, published extracts from his collection as a double CD entitled *Blagdon and Mendip Voices*. It is a unique oral history and makes a valuable contribution to our local knowledge. The Society was pleased to support this venture using a portion of our grant from the Heritage Lottery Fund.

Although each author makes his or her acknowledgement of any help they may have received, the Society's thanks are also due to the work and expertise of the Somerset Vernacular Building Research Group (SVBRG). The group has carried out surveys of approximately eight of the older houses in the village, by a careful systematic analysis of the surviving fabric supplemented by any available written evidence. The aim is to provide a sound basis for the likely date the buildings were erected and subsequently altered over the centuries. This research has helped to restore the balance of the evidence rather than some of the more fanciful claims to antiquity that have been promulgated in the past. This work was funded through the generosity of the Heritage Lottery Fund.

The Society's thanks are due to Mrs Mead and family for all their support, to David and Anne Lock for sharing their extensive collection of Blagdon photographs and memorabilia, to Frank and Sue Fronckowiak for the thoughful gift of a reel to reel recording machine, to the Society's members for all their help, to Dr Peter King and Olga Shotton for their assistance with the proof reading, and to Sheila Johnson for IT support in producing these volumes. We are very grateful for the support of Graham and Johanna Brown for selling our publications in Blagdon Village Stores and also to Malcolm and Sheila Brown for sales via the Village Club. Finally we would like to thank the Heritage Lottery Fund and the Nationwide Building Society for their generous grants which make it all possible.

Dr Neil Bentham
Editor, BLHS, August 2007

The Development of Blagdon

John Chamberlain

Introduction

Having been directly involved in a great many of the building projects which have taken place in Blagdon during the past sixty or more years I have had the good fortune to gain an in-depth knowledge of at least forty dwellings in the village, many on sites of considerable antiquity. From my participation during student days as a builder's 'mate' to acting professionally in an advisory capacity on conservation, listing and restoration of buildings in the locality for District and County Councils, it would be very easy either to consider a number of older buildings in greater detail or to provide an extended commentary on the development of the village in the second half of the twentieth century. I have therefore endeavoured to maintain a relatively broad brush approach to the overall development of the village, especially as in recent years so much has been recorded for the archive by the Recent History Group.

ભ   ભ   ભ   ભ   ભ

There is a wealth of evidence of very early occupation in surrounding parishes: Aveline's Hole and Read's Cavern[1] in Burrington, Row of Ashes at Butcombe, Fairy Toot near Nempnett Thrubwell, the stone circle at Stanton Drew and the circles and tumuli on Mendip, but to date no comparable indication of occupation has been established in Blagdon. The boundaries of the old Saxon parish of Blagdon are well established, particularly on the east and west, by virtue of the 'lost' charter of Ubley and the surviving Wrington charter. To the north, with an anomaly to include Aldwick, the boundary was marked by the River Yeo. However the southern boundary, although always including parts of Charterhouse, has been less well defined.

A logical division of land along the northern slopes of Mendip forming the parishes of East and West Harptree, Compton Martin, Ubley, Blagdon, Burrington, Wrington and beyond is linked by a broadly east–west track system. Similar routes run north from Charterhouse through Blagdon to Butcombe and Redhill. It has been suggested that in each of the Yeo Valley Mendip villages there could be a Roman villa sited in every Saxon parish but it is, of course, possible that the Saxon parishes were formed as a legacy from the government of the time of Roman occupation.

The Saxon influence was of great significance in the development of Blagdon from the naming of the settlement (Saxon Blaec Dun meaning Bleak Hill) to other names such as Merecombe (meaning valley boundary) still in use to-day.

Much of the Saxon western parish boundary can still be followed in the description of the Saxon charter which shows the importance of the Rickford spring and the formation of the settlement of Ellick with, by implication, "old" Swymmers[2] (which was located approximately 200m southeast of the present Swymmers Farm). Whilst these are "outliers" to the village itself they give a clue to the possible development of settlements within Blagdon. These developments occur between the springline to the north and the areas of upland woodlands which occupy steeply sloping and often broken ground to the south. The springline is still apparent and the woodland remains almost unbroken, but often replanted, from East Harptree to Churchill. There is some evidence that areas of this woodland could be that classified as 'ancient' by Rackham and others[3].

The continuance of the hamlet of Rickford should be noted. It is reasonably certain that one of the two mills mentioned in the Domesday survey subsisted in close proximity to the powerful spring, although it was not until the end of the nineteenth century that the relatively extensive amount of building now seen in Rickford began to appear. In mediaeval times one of the more important routes from Rickford was likely to be via Leg Lane eastward to the top of Hook's Batch and then to Blagdon. This would avoid the marshy spring-fed ground now known as Blagdon Coombe. The enclosures, Millwoods[4] (forming part of the pumping station grounds), suggests the location of the second Blagdon mill. The River Yeo and its tributaries sustained at least three other mills between Millwoods, Butcombe, Ubley and Compton Martin.

The status of Mendip as a Royal forest dates from Saxon times with origins in the parishes of Cheddar and Axbridge. In this context the word 'forest' does not relate to woodland but refers to land used by the king as a royal hunting ground. The area in question later extended to include the whole of the Mendip Hills and, therefore, part of the parish of Blagdon. Although the outlying areas of Ellick/"old" Swymmers and the hamlets of Rickford and Aldwick are all part of the Saxon parish of Blagdon, the main settlement of the village of Blagdon is the principal subject of the following topic of development.

At a guess, we should find evidence of Saxon habitation around the areas of Coombe Lodge, Court Farm/Bell Square/Village Club and the Church Street location: there could have been some habitation at Merecombe and probably in the vicinities of Wadley and Holt Farms (fig.1). It is likely that they were a continuation of much earlier agricultural foundations which also assisted in provisioning the mining community on Mendip. Primarily due to the relatively broken nature of the landscape these groups were scattered over a wide area to make the most of available shelter, sun and springs (water). Together with the added benefits of good but piecemeal soil conditions and the fact that areas of high ground, particularly above Rudgen, command overviews for a considerable distance, the prevailing conditions gave rise to a settlement which does not conform to the generally accepted pattern of village development.

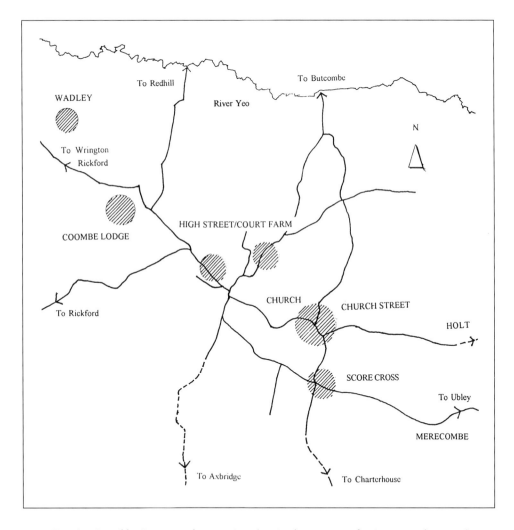

Fig. 1 - Possible Saxon settlement sites (set in the context of existing road pattern)

It is more than likely that there was a Saxon church on or near the site of the present building, particularly if following earlier Roman occupation. The combination of religious site above a near-by spring[5] is a common one along the northern slope of Mendip and one linking conveniently with the ancient way through the village. It is known that Alfred, from his base at Wedmore, fought battles successfully against the Danes in the old Hundred of Winterstoke around Blagdon. There are a number of fields (running south above Clander's corner) called Bloodyfield within the settlement which may, or may not, be of significance as such names normally indicate areas where battles were fought. As a Romano Christian he, or his officers, would almost certainly have had access to a place of worship nearby.

Any such church of this time would be very basic – more than likely to be quite simple and of framed timber construction. Dwellings, on the other hand, were primarily much smaller in scale, constructed of wooden posts, wattle, daub and thatch, in the form of modest single-storey buildings with rudimentary hearths and little or no chimney construction.

Moving to the Domesday record, we know that Serlo de Burci held estates in Dorset and Somerset, including Blagdon. Subsequently the majority of the estates passed to the Martin family under the general title of the Barony of Blagdon. Again, the division of lands is unclear but what is certain is that general ownership of lands in the parish became divided – the eastern half being primarily ecclesiastic, the western secular. There is no evidence of a Norman church replacing any Saxon place of worship, but the existence of a stone piscina possibly dating from this time and the strange stone tablet incorporated in the south face of the present tower indicates some earlier permanent structure. At this time arable (ploughed) land comprises 1,000 acres; pasture and meadowland 650 acres; woodland 200 acres and 'domestic' 200 acres – a total of some 2050 acres. The absence of any established Norman buildings in the village suggests that such dwellings as there were continued in the simple Saxon manner, with some clad in local stone. They would still be single storey construction extended to provide a smoke bay or some other form of rudimentary fireplace or chimney breast construction. Many of these early dwellings became the site of or provided the foundation for later forms of construction. These groups of dwellings became the basis for the layout of the village as it exists to-day.

The individual groups were connected by tracks, or ways, which in turn provided access to and from the village (fig. 2). These developed into the "hollow ways" of which there are still examples, although a number are no longer readily evident – Dark Lane and Score Lane are the only present examples which are easily visible. Hollow ways were often relatively deep depressions formed by continuous usage and erosion of the land surface. Their depth and extent is variable and governed by geological conditions arising from outcrops of rock, inclination of land surface and other factors. Many of the original hollow ways are now concealed by the high stone walls which are a feature of the present Blagdon landscape. It is easy to imagine parts of Station Road, High Street and parts of Church Street with much narrower tracks and high earth banks where to-day there are made up roads and retaining stone walls. The continuation of Grib Lane (The Grib) was once a hollow way of similar dimensions to Dark Lane. The western approach to the village from Bourne Lane also contains several elements of hollow way. The geological conditions dictated that some ways were cut into the shoulders of the land. A good example is at Dipland where the original course of the road can be seen to the south of Dipland Batch.

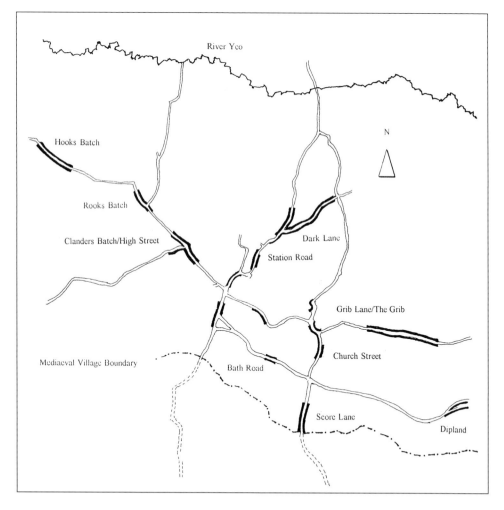

Fig. 2. - Early routes through, to and from village
location of "hollow ways" shown in thicker line

From 1260 onwards the powers of feudal courts over freeholders declined, although the administrative changes which occurred had little effect at local level and during the mediaeval period there is little direct evidence of development. Small fragments, such as coinage[6] and shards of pottery, and a little documentary evidence suggest a continuing and possibly expanding community. The predominantly timber constructions of the Saxon period were progressively replaced and extended. Stone would have been the material of choice for the church which, in 1292, is recorded as being 'valued at twenty-five marks'. In the early 1960s, during the course of renovation works of the northern cottages in Bell Square[7], timber framing of cruck form was revealed with a possible dating of 1380-1400 (of very similar construction as found during later renovation of Church Cottage, Backwell[8]). Other than use as roofing material timber was gradually replaced by local stone for construction of dwellings, evidence for which appears in Stone's and King's Cottages, Court Farmhouse and in several buildings around the Church. Thatch, using reed from the valley bottom, covered the roofs of the majority of dwellings. Typical stages in development of a dwelling are shown in fig. 3.

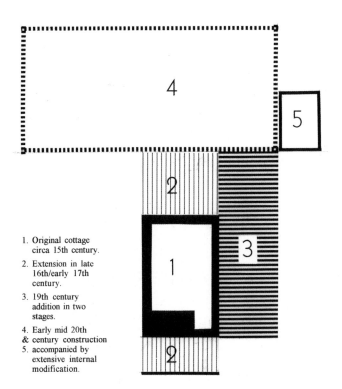

1. Original cottage circa 15th century.
2. Extension in late 16th/early 17th century.
3. 19th century addition in two stages.
4. Early mid 20th & century construction
5. accompanied by extensive internal modification.

Fig. 3 - Typical stages in the development of a Blagdon property.

The original cottage probably had a makeshift partition to provide two "rooms" at ground floor level and a ladder stair to an open attic above

It is not a simple matter to put an accurate date on the construction of many buildings unless firm evidence is available from legal documents. It was often many years before styles of construction and building details as practised in towns and cities were taken up in rural areas. Dating by dendrochronology can be similarly misleading unless it is certain that the timbers in question have been in situ from the time of first use and not 'recycled' from elsewhere. Re-use of materials has always been common practice and Blagdon is no exception. There are many instances of re-using timber components originally used elsewhere.

It was not until the fifteenth century that trading classes began to take precedence. Sheep-farming and the consequent production of wool was particularly important to Mendip and Blagdon and this, together with rising prosperity in agriculture and the increasing importance of the proximity of Bristol, consolidated the status of the village. The present church tower dates from the end of the fifteenth century, a period which saw the rebuilding of many of the North Somerset towers. These are said to be the work of a travelling company of master masons, although the few masons' marks still evident in the Blagdon tower do not necessarily support this view. The status of the village can be gauged from the quality of the church tower and from artefacts of the period such as the misericords and screen removed in a later re-build. It is during this period that the alternative route from High Street via Bath Road to the top of Church Street began to gain prominence. Dwellings were becoming more sophisticated although remaining small in scale. A good example is the northernmost range of building at The New Inn (fig.4).

Fig. 4 - The New Inn, showing comparison of small scale late 16th century dwelling and adjoining larger 18th/19th century building – both on sites of earlier structures (David Lock)

In common with other parishes in England, by the middle of the sixteenth century the church in Blagdon was undertaking a role of formally recorded administration of the parish. There are registers of baptisms, marriages and burials dating from 1555 and detailed records of churchwardens' accounts, receipts and charity disbursements, overseers' accounts, maintenance of the poor, administration of the poor house and apprentices, and Rates and Assessments. The Blagdon records are very full and, fortunately, almost intact[9]. They include the endowment of Thomas Baynard, who in 1687 founded the Baynard Trust: Blagdon was probably the only village in the Mendips to benefit from such an unusual charitable educational foundation, which led to the establishment of Blagdon Primary School.

The woollen trade and its associated activities – growing of teazles and fulling of cloth – had flourished, but a decline during the early part of the sixteenth century was to some extent offset by the mining boom on Mendip which was at its height by 1700. Blagdon was one of the few villages along the northern slope of Mendip in which little, if any, mining activity took place. However, there is one recorded mine within the old Saxon parish boundary – an isolated and very small working slightly to the north of the present wood-shavings factory at Charterhouse[10]. It is from this time that the consolidation of the Street End settlement, generally believed to be associated with the mining industry, is most likely to date. It is certainly above and beyond the mediaeval southern boundary of the village and originally founded on common land. These cottages were extremely small, much more closely grouped than elsewhere in the village and hastily constructed, primarily sited to take greatest advantage of the shelter afforded by the shoulder of the hill.

Throughout the eighteenth century modest changes occurred in the structures of the village with many properties undergoing progressive improvements. In general this upgrading of property was part of a continuing system of development which occurred during periods of prosperity throughout the centuries. The nature and extent of alteration was determined by the circumstances of the owner for the time being. In the case of Coombe Lodge extension of the homestead was undertaken on a significant scale, including re-ordering of the grounds and woodland, culminating in the house occupied by Thomas Rowarth in the 1840s – the only house in the village at that time described as a mansion. By the end of the first quarter of the nineteenth century other comparatively substantial houses in the village such as Blagdon Court and the Rectory (now the Old Rectory) had also been improved but on a smaller scale.

Whilst the first Act of Parliament relating to the formation of the West Harptree Turnpike Trust came into force in 1793, it was not until the end of the second decade of the nineteenth century that the revision and upgrading of the road system through Blagdon began to take effect. This led to the consolidation of Bath Road as the major east-west route and the formation of a made-up road through the Coombe to Rickford. It is likely that this road forded the spring at Rickford (bridge) but to date there is no evidence to confirm this[11]. The location of the Blagdon toll house shows that the custodian had care of two gates, one controlling the 'main' (Bath) road, the other the entry to the toll road from Butcombe and Nempnett Thrubwell. There is a surviving toll board showing toll charges (fig.5). At this time roads were still very rudimentary – largely formed of hand-compacted stone and gravel and often deeply rutted. The parish, that is the Church authorities, had responsibility for administration of tolls for the turnpike trust and the care of side roads. The removal of the turnpike is noted in the Vestry minutes between March and December 1875, when it was proposed that the parish keep the turnpike roads in the same state of repair as left by the turnpike trust.

A major change in the pattern of the landscape was brought about by the Enclosure Act of 1795 with the formation of field systems in the southern part of the parish. The Newfields area had already been divided and enclosed before this time and formed a more structured and regular field pattern to that which existed elsewhere in the parish. Both these enclosures marked a significant point of development in the agriculture of the area, although the newly enclosed land lying above the 700ft contour implied farming techniques which differed from those in the valley floor. Of necessity such enclosures led to the provision of more buildings and modest farmsteads of varying types were built on Mendip from locally available materials, although the buildings were not always of particularly good quality. The Act also provided land above Street End for the parish quarry.

However, in the village of Blagdon one of the most significant building projects in the first part of the nineteenth century was the rebuilding of the main body of St Andrew's Church in 1823, after the Church Building Act of 1818 had provided one million pounds to spend on building churches throughout the country. The tower escaped rebuilding but was amended internally to provide easy access to a "a singing gallery," a prominent feature complete with cast iron columns. A new south aisle extended the original nave/north aisle footprint. Much of the material from the "old" building was sold, as were many of the internal fixtures and fittings.

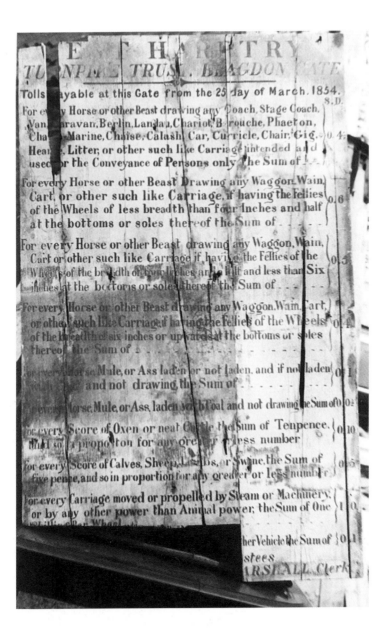

Fig. 5 - Toll Board from the Blagdon Tollhouse found in the floor of Andrew Addicott's house in Bell Square. Photograph – BLHS Archive, the Toll Board is the property of Andrew Addicott

The tithe map and roll of 1842 together give an in depth analysis of housing, owners and tenants and the agricultural make-up of the parish (fig. 6). In the village itself, including the Rickford hamlet, there were 182 dwellings on the roll. Twenty six of those dwellings have now totally vanished and of the remainder many have been substantially extended or modified in some way. Although some dwellings were listed without gardens there were a number of "garden plots" in individual ownership which were noted separately.

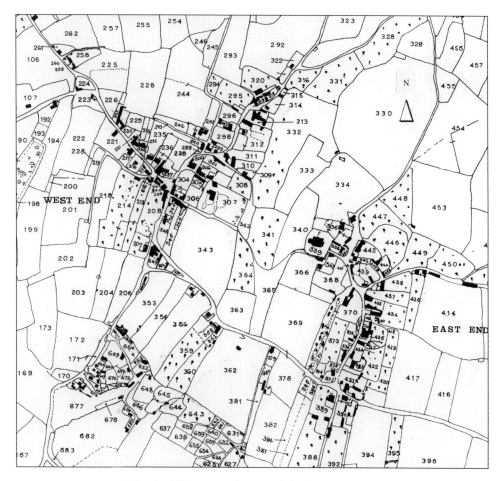

Fig. 6. - The principal areas of development of the village copied from the tithe map of 1842

The roll also contained notes of property at Aldwick, where there were five dwellings including The Court together with outbuildings specifically described as "ox houses". Interestingly, no ox houses were mentioned within Blagdon. Property in the parish was in a considerable number of ownerships but with few extensive land and building holdings. More than 100 properties were tenanted and a number of the more significant property owners were women. An additional sixteen dwellings were in the ownership of the Blagdon Overseers of the Poor (the parish). Blagdon School was rebuilt at this time and again extended before the end of the century. Responsibility for administering the parish was gradually passing from the Church to civil authorities, although this process was not complete until the twentieth century.

Although there was no single large landowner two families, the Seymours and the Stephens, each owned over 450 acres, comprising buildings, fields and woodland in small tenanted parcels and distributed throughout the parish. Access to these disparate parcels of land was achieved in many ways without apparent recourse to wayleaves. In addition to the Rector for the time being six other reverend gentlemen owned property and/or land in the parish but not all were resident. The Rector, or his curate, occupied The Rectory (now The Old Rectory) adjacent to the Glebe lands. The use of land recorded in the Tithe Roll shows remarkably little variation to that noted in the Domesday survey. Subsequent to the 1842 Tithe Roll the small Coombe Lodge estate (fig. 7) passed from Thomas Rowarth to Captain and Mrs Valpy and in 1879/80 was purchased by W.H. Wills. This marked the beginning of perhaps the most radical development of the village.

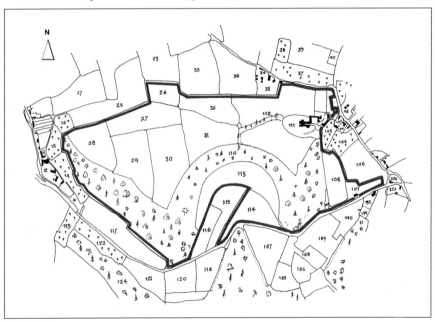

Fig. 7- The extent of the Coombe Lodge Estate from the 1842 tithe map showing parts of the earlier 18th century landscape to the east of the mansion and before the later landscaping and further planting of the Coombe

The industrial revolution of the nineteenth century had led to the migration of many who worked in rural occupations to towns and cities with the consequent growth of housing and commerce. It was not uncommon for those who had prospered from the trade and industry of city life to turn their attentions towards improving the quality of life in the countryside, one effect of which was the introduction of "model" villages.

Having purchased Coombe Lodge, W.H. Wills first established a small nucleus of buildings in the Menlea area to support the estate, which included a dairy, laundry, generator house, stables and cottages. Additional facilities in the form of shops, the Village Club and further housing extended throughout the village, all designed in a characteristic "model" village style by an architect relative, Frank Wills, who also acted as Agent to the estate.

In all approximately fifty new houses were built at this time, primarily to accommodate estate workers and their families. Over a period W.H. Wills acquired some 1500 acres of land within the parish to create the Coombe Lodge estate. He had considerable interests in agriculture and agricultural improvement and by 1910 these 1500 or so acres were divided into separate lots of roughly 100 acres, each with its own farmhouse and ancillary buildings. Most were newly built with little conversion of existing properties.

During the same period Bristol Waterworks also acquired land and farmsteads in both Blagdon and adjoining parishes in association with construction works for Blagdon Lake. A large pumping station was built in the valley bottom together with an Engineer's house and an 'Inspector's' house. This large dwelling, complete with caretakers' accommodation, was also used by Directors of the Company, initially to view the progress of the works and later to act as a base for the inspection of the Company's assets in the area. Closer to the village itself three pairs of employees' cottages were erected. Mains drainage was introduced by the Company both within the village and along the southern boundary of the lake, together with a very limited water supply. Over a number of years there was a considerable increase in population in the village in association with the building of the lake, as evidenced in the 1901 census, with a similar increase in the number of pupils attending school. Much of the employment was of a temporary nature but some permanent employment ensued.

The Wrington Vale Light Railway serving Langford, Burrington and Blagdon opened at the end of 1901 but the proposal to extend eastward to the Somerset coalfield never materialised. A Baptist Chapel was built in 1875 and an adjacent hall some nine years later. By 1907, the Methodist Chapel (which replaced the earlier Wesleyan chapel on Bath Road), hall and caretaker's house had been constructed as a gift by Sidney Hill of Langford. W.H. Wills restored the tower of the parish church in 1896 and made provision for casting a completely new peal of eight bells in 1902 (to commemorate the coronation of that year in all probability.) With the exception of the tower, the parish church of St Andrew was again rebuilt between 1908 and 1910: at the same time a Parish Room was provided for divine worship during the period of construction, all at the expense of W.H. Wills.

These nineteenth and early twentieth century interventions did little to integrate further the existing basic village structure. With the exception of the Wills' Estate and Bristol Waterworks Company's housing, comparatively little new housing was constructed during the early part of the twentieth century (fig. 8). However, with the advent of a perceived trend for healthy 'rural' living and motorised transport more generally available, it became almost fashionable to build houses in slightly more remote locations such as Ellick Road and Newfields. Within the village itself some local authority housing was proposed in the mid 1920s and various sites for the construction of ten or twelve houses considered by the Parish Council. Land was subsequently made available by the major landowner and six pairs of houses were built at Dipland by 1930. By this time "old" Coombe Lodge had been demolished and a new house, designed in the traditional country house style by Sir George Oatley, constructed in its place. Although the largest domestic dwelling ever to be built in the parish of Blagdon, Coombe Lodge was in use for only thirty years as a private residence.

Fig. 8 - Looking down Score Lane from 'The Score' towards East End c1930.
The thatched cottages at the head of Score Lane were still inhabited as late as the 1930s.
(Olga Shotton)

Immediately after 1945 the Parish Council made strenuous efforts to increase the housing stock within the village. Account was also taken of the need to provide housing on the top of Mendip and also ensure that this part of the parish was provided with a mains water supply. Building materials were rationed and construction restricted by licence. It was not until 1949 that any real progress was made and local authority funded housing provided at Boyd's Orchard (Garston Lane), at East Croft and West Croft (Score Lane) (fig. 9).

Fig. 9 - Postwar housing under construction in East Croft (Olga Shotton)

Construction work was undertaken by C.F. Payne, a Blagdon builder who provided a major source of employment within the village – a radical change from the agricultural and estate-based employment of the between-war years. These developments, although significant, still maintained the major groupings of East End, West End, Street End and Menlea.

A very limited amount of private development took place off Liberty Lane and several individual houses were built in various parts of the village. There was no major private development until the construction of the Fallowfield estate in the early 1960s, in part built on land originally used as the village allotments. This consolidated the West End/Street End village structure. Further subsequent small groups of housing were located in Garston Lane/Station Road, the Score Lane area and Church Street, in addition to individual plots. Small cottages were enlarged: in some instances a single unit was converted from two small cottages.

In the second half of the twentieth century more than 200 new houses were built. Although between 1842 and the end of the twentieth century the number of dwellings had more than doubled, the population remained virtually the same (Figs. 10a, 10b, 10c).

In comparatively few years the rapid increase in housing stock placed severe demands on both water supply and other services. The original public mains drainage system, laid as part of the formation of the lake, was extremely limited. One reason was undoubtedly the high costs incurred as a result of the rocky nature and varying levels of ground within the village. The system was subsequently extended in a piecemeal fashion over some thirty years by agreement between Axbridge Rural District Council and Bristol Waterworks Company. Mains water distribution was also undertaken in similar fashion: some properties in the village were not served by public mains until 1969.

The introduction of electricity, first proposed to serve the village in 1929, followed a similar but overground pattern. Some houses were not connected to the supply until the early 1940s with outlying properties still reliant on alternative forms of lighting for a further ten or so years. By 1927 telephones had arrived – one of the first (number 2) was for the Bristol Waterworks' Engineer. The original small manual exchange in the Post Office was superseded by an automatic exchange located at the Mead and eventually replaced by the present building near the fire station. A gas supply was not introduced until toward the end of the twentieth century.

By the late 1960s much employment in rural areas was no longer locally based: the era of the commuter had arrived. The Bristol Waterworks Company had disposed of the farmland originally acquired before construction of the lake and the farms returned to 'private' ownership. Over comparatively few years farming practices also changed: many of the Estate small farm units were no longer viable and, whilst the farmland was retained, the farmhouses became private residential dwellings; many farm buildings were converted into residential, holiday and commercial units. The number of tenanted farm holdings was significantly reduced.

These changes also affected land in other ownerships. As land became available it was incorporated into larger holdings. Together with the change in use of Coombe Lodge and the expansion of the Holt Farm/Yeo Valley enterprises, within forty years opportunities for employment in the area were increased significantly.

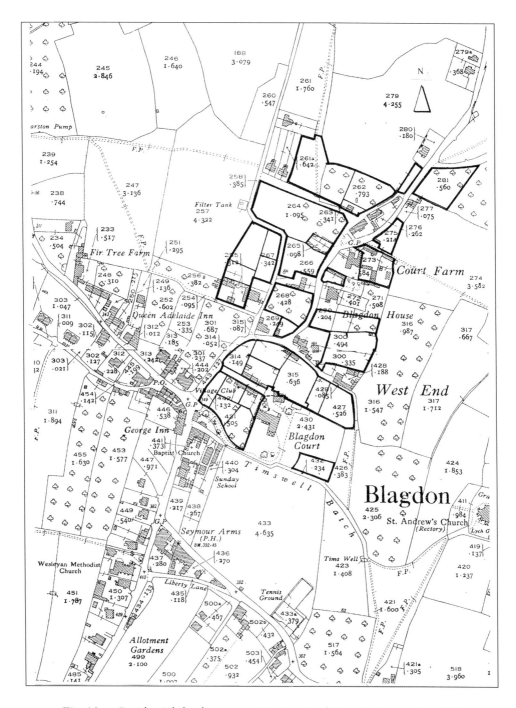

*Fig. 10a - Residential development in Station Road/Garston Lane after 1950
(underlying map from OS Somerset LXVIII.3 1931)*

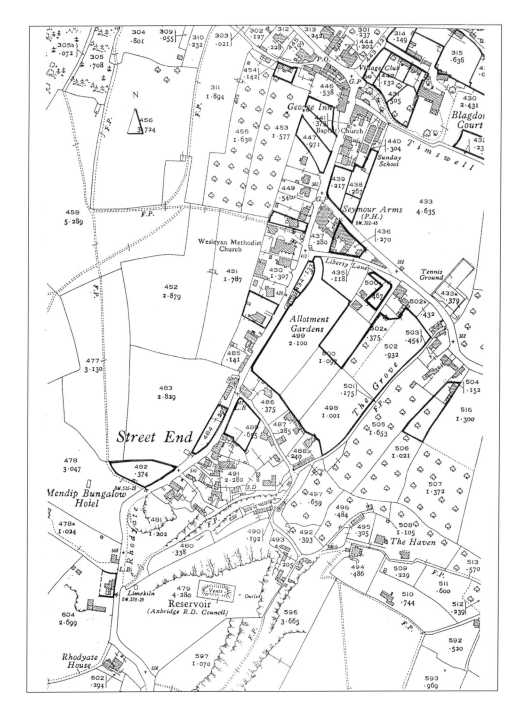

*Fig. 10b - Residential development in High Street / Street End after 1950
(underlying map from O.S. Somerset LXVIII.7 1931)*

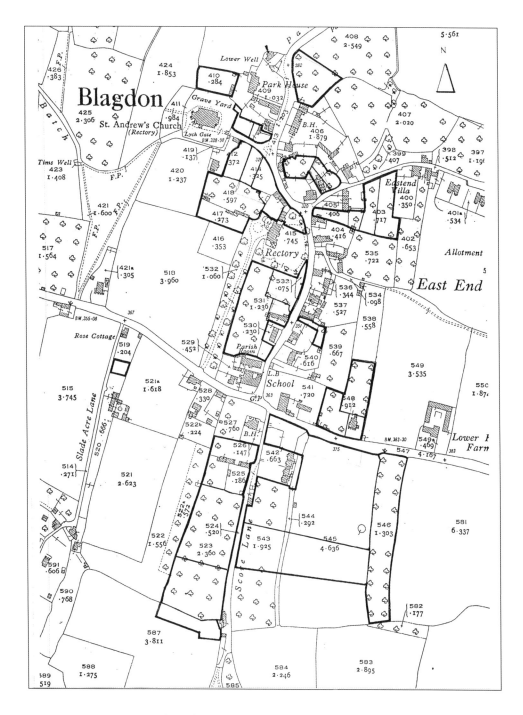

*Fig. 10c - Residential development in Score Lane/East End after 1950
(underlying map from O.S. Somerset LXVIII.7 1931)*

With the alteration in county boundaries in 1974 the civil boundary of the village changed dramatically. The southern part of Blagdon parish, formerly in Axbridge Rural District Council, was transferred to the newly formed Mendip District Council in Somerset. The overall size of the civil parish was reduced by an adjustment in the southern boundary to the newly formed Woodspring District Council in the new county of Avon. A further reduction in the size of the civil parish took place around the turn of the 20th and 21st centuries when the hamlet of Rickford was transferred to Burrington parish. The county of Avon 'disappeared' and Blagdon became a parish in North Somerset District. The ecclesiastical parish maintains the original Saxon boundary.

The general landscape and overall visual appearance of the parish has seen many changes. Common land to the south has been enclosed; the River Yeo was dammed to form a lake; the churchyard was extended westward in the early part of the twentieth century and the footpath which once crossed the churchyard was diverted to its present line. The enlarged churchyard provided the final resting place for many from the Nordrach Sanatorium and space soon became a problem. In the mid 1950s a new (civil) parish cemetery was provided at the end of Grib Lane. The orchards once abundant throughout the village together with those adjoining public houses have disappeared: there are no longer mature elm trees, once so prominent at the (old) Rectory and in the valley hedgerows. The main A368 was widened and 'straightened' between The Grove and Slad Acre Lane and at the same time a footpath was created which extended as far as the School. Eldred's Orchard, a new parish orchard with trees donated by parishioners, was planted toward the end of the twentieth century on land acquired by the Parish Council to replace an orchard which had virtually disappeared.

Bibliography

ATTHILL, Robin	*The Curious Past.* (Wessex Press, 1955)
	Old Mendip. (David & Charles/MacDonald,1964)
ATTHILL, Robin (Editor)	*Mendip: A New Study.* (David & Charles, 1976)
BOARD, M.E.	*Blagdon on Mendip: Traditions and Records.* (1947)
BOND, James	*Somerset Parks & Gardens* (Somerset Books, 1998)
CLARK Sir Kenneth KCB	*The Gothic Revival* (Constable, 1928, revised 1950)
COLLINSON, The Rev. John	*The History of Somersetshire.* Volume III (Crutwell Printers, Bath, 1793)
COWARD, Mary	*Rickford: A History of a North Somerset Village* (Millennium Festival Awards, 2000)
FIELD, John	*English Field Names* (Alan Sutton, 1989)
	A History of English Field Names (Longman, 1993)
GOUGH, James W. MA DLitt	*The Mines of Mendip* (David & Charles, 1967)
HADDON, John B.A.	*Notes on "The Mendip Country with Special Reference to Blagdon* (University of Bristol, 1959)
HEWETT, Cecil A	*English Historic Carpentry* (Phillimore & Co Ltd 1980)
MASON, R.T.	*Framed Buildings of England* (Coach House Publishing, 1974)
RACKHAM, Oliver	*History of the Countryside* (George Weidenfield & Nicholson, 1994)
ROSS, Lesley (Ed)	*Before the Lake* (The Harptree History Society, 2004)
WATSON, S.J.	*Furnished with Ability* (Michael Russell, 1991)

---

[1] Peter Johnson, The History of Mendip Caving (David & Charles, 1967)

[2] Correspondence with Francis Neale – author's archive,

[3] Author's notes and records,

[4] 1842 Tithe Map and Roll – copies in author's possession.

[5] A similar example exists at Compton Martin.

[6] In author's collection.

[7] Work undertaken under the direction of Coffin, Jones & Roden, architects & surveyors, Bristol and Weston-super-Mare.

[8] Renovation and report undertaken for Woodspring District Council (author).

[9] Documents lodged with Somerset County Record Office, Taunton.

[10] J.W. Gough, *The Mines of Mendip*, p.253. Probably the working noted by Catcott in 1756, a shaft first sunk in an attempt to find coal.

[11] The possibility of providing a bridge over the Rickford brook at Bourne was still being discussed by Blagdon Parish Council in 1926.

Hannah More and her connections with Blagdon, part two: the "Blagdon Controversy" 1798-1802

Elizabeth M. Harvey

Note on sources and background: Words in italics are from primary sources. The most important primary sources, which have only survived in printed form, are Thomas Bere's *Controversy between Mrs[1] Hannah More and the Curate of Blagdon,* published in 1801; Thomas Whalley's correspondence with Hannah More, published by his nephew in 1863; and *The Anti-Jacobin Review.* More's original correspondence with William Wilberforce is included in the Wilberforce Papers at Duke University, North Carolina, but some of this correspondence was published by William Roberts. Part One of this essay provides background, including the creation and early years of the Blagdon Sunday school, and can be found in *A History of Blagdon, Volume 2.*

The "Blagdon Controversy," as it came to be known, began in the autumn of 1798 as a dispute between Hannah More and Thomas Bere, the curate of Blagdon, over the behaviour of her Sunday school teacher, Henry Young. In 1801 the dispute was taken up nationally and was discussed at dinner tables in London and beyond. Both sides rallied supporters and, although Bere initially seemed to have the upper hand, his supporters gradually deserted him and Hannah More ultimately recovered her reputation. How and why apparently trivial events on the Mendips came to be presented in journals as events of national significance can only be understood in the religious and political context of the late 18th century.

Opposition to the Wedmore School[2]

In May 1798, when the More sisters returned from Bath to their summer home at Cowslip Green, they found *great peaceableness* [in Blagdon village, and their school] *in a good state of improvement.* [The adults at the evening reading all] *stood up, and, with the modesty and simplicity of children, suffered the master to stand forward and state to* [them] *the particulars of their behaviour during the winter.* [Mr Bere also wished the sisters] *to be publicly informed of the extraordinary decorum of the men on the day of their club, which had just taken place* [so the sisters concluded] *that religion was evidently operating upon their conduct, and were much rejoiced at it.*

That summer the sisters had two young guests at their cottage in Cowslip Green: Thomas Fry and James Vaughan were both Evangelical Oxford graduates in their early twenties. Like the Mores, they were Evangelicals within the Established Church.[3] The *zeal of these young men is extremely delightful*, Patty More[4] wrote in her journal after Fry and Vaughan returned from Wedmore, determined that the sisters should open a school in that populous and wicked place. Despite opposition from a wealthy local farmer, who had declared that the day *the school was opened would be the beginning of such rebellion in England as had taken place in Ireland and France*, a Sunday school was opened in Wedmore. Many Mendip farmers believed that educating the poor would make them dissatisfied; they would lose respect for their superiors; and this would lead to revolt. While Mr Fry and the schoolmaster were teaching a hymn to the children, another angry farmer cried out: *Oh sir, I am afraid this must be Methody* [Methodism] which Fry denied, as he was *a clergyman of the Church of England*. The Wedmore farmers had highlighted the two issues which became central to the "Blagdon Controversy": religion and politics or, more specifically, Methodism and Radicalism. Soon both the Wedmore and Axbridge schools were accused of *enthusiasm*[5] and Mr Bere became worried about the school in Blagdon.

Soon after this Mr Bere visited Axbridge and *preached a daring sermon openly against the Trinity;*[6] *and not content with this, did the same in his own parish, and indirectly preached against the school. The whole parish was thrown into confusion, and from a full school, and considerably above two hundred at the evening reading, it all at once fell off to thirty-five.* Hannah and Patty went to Blagdon, *called the people together, and* [Hannah] *made a long speech to them, threatening to take away the school, if an immediate alteration did not take place. A religious farmer confessed that the terror of the people was very great, fearing to offend* [Mr Bere, who was also a magistrate, and] *ruled them with a rod of iron.* [The sisters] *taxed him with his own letters of approbation which* [they] *had from time to time received … and he was brought again to confess before witnesses the extraordinary benefit the school had been to the parish* [so] *the school and reading filled again rapidly.*

However, during the winter, opposition to the Wedmore school revived and news of this reached Blagdon where *Satan was busy, through the instrumentality of him who called himself a preacher of the gospel … Malicious tales were advanced, and the master here, likewise, was cruelly misrepresented as an enthusiast, and as misleading the minds of the people. Some uneasy letters passed upon the subject, in reference to both parishes.*

Henry Young's private Monday evening school[7]

In 1796 Mr Bere had considered the Blagdon schoolmaster to be a *clever and useful man*[8] but, in the autumn of 1798, he and his wife, Sarah, became concerned about the private school meetings which the schoolmaster, Henry Young, held at the school on Monday evenings. While the sisters were in Bath, Mrs Bere and two friends attended one of these meetings at Hannah's suggestion. In January Mrs Bere wrote to Hannah that the children were making great improvement in the Sunday School and that many people attended on Sunday evenings to hear the sermon. Then she described the Monday evening school, which opened with singing and prayers:

> *There were 13 or 14 of the usual attendants assembled, when Mr Young opened the conversation, with observing what persecutions he had suffered ever since he had been walking in the ways of the Lord, which was about fourteen years. After this he began to interrogate the people, singly relative to their spiritual state; to which they individually replied with comfortable confidence. When this examination was over, Mr Young said this was what they called their private school, and if anyone mentioned what transpired he never desired to see them again. When the people were dismissed, I observed to Mr Young that these were a very happy set of people indeed, if they did not deceive themselves, which I hoped they did not. He seemed hurt by my observation, and replied, there was no danger of that. I told him, I hoped not, but I feared, if the like questions had been put to me, I could not have given such satisfactory answers as they had all done. Mr Young said, perhaps Madam, you have not sought the Lord the same way they have.*

Mrs Bere was surprised that there were no extempore prayers,[9] which she had heard was the usual practice, and suggested to Hannah that, *if Mr Young pursued the original plan of publicly reading to them, and with them, the holy scriptures and using the excellent forms of prayer,* which Hannah had given him for the purpose, then there would be less *danger of falling into that deplorable state.*

It wasn't easy for Hannah to control her schoolteachers when she was in Bath and, as she was very ill that winter, she asked Patty to speak to Henry Young about his evening school, which resembled a Methodist meeting. Young's irregularities apparently ended but, as Hannah didn't reply to Mrs Bere's letter until April, the Beres felt slighted and Mr Bere concluded that Hannah *had no violent objection to her school being so conducted.*

In May 1799, when the sisters returned to Cowslip Green, Patty wrote in her journal: *In spite of all the sneers and malevolence at Blagdon, yet the scene, on our first visit, was deeply interesting – a fine, well-constructed, orderly school, and a very comfortable, though not large, evening reading.* However, many adults were afraid of Mr Bere and had stopped attending the reading.[10] When Hannah told Mr Bere that she had heard he preached a sermon against the school, he replied: *Something, madam, relative to enthusiasm, but nothing against the school.* In June the Beres spent a week with Dr Crossman, the absentee[11] Rector of Blagdon, who was also Rector of West Monkton near Taunton. As the Crossmans spent the summers in West Monkton and the winters in Bath, they rarely visited Blagdon, so Mr Bere took the opportunity to mention Mr Young's private school and Mrs Bere's letter to Hannah More.[12]

A loose, silly lad and a baronet[13]

Blagdon was suspiciously quiet that summer and Patty wrote in her journal: *Blagdon is doing so well, and in such a happy state at the end of 1799, that, knowing the uncertainty of all human events, we tremble over its very prosperity.* They were right to tremble for, at the beginning of 1800, *a violent explosion, long pent up, took place at Blagdon. The curate and justice no longer concealed the cloven foot but broke out in a great fury against poor Younge[14] … by getting a loose, silly lad to swear a false oath to the prejudice of his character. H and I were both in London when this unpleasant event took place. Bere's letter, accompanying the case against Younge, was short and impudent, desiring the dismissal of the master immediately, without allowing him time to plead his own cause.*[15]

The *loose, silly lad* was Silas Derrick, who had recently become a servant at the parsonage, which was then Blagdon House in Butcombe Road – now Station Road. Silas had sworn an affidavit before S.T. Wylde, a local magistrate and Vicar of Burrington, in which he claimed that Henry Young had said: *I would not advise you to go to service at Mr Bere's at all, and if you do go, I would not advise you to stay there long – for there is no knowing what they may put in your mind, to make you sign away your rights to the house and orchard.* This property was occupied by his mother, Sarah. Silas, who held the property in mortgage, stated that they *were never directly or indirectly mentioned to* him by Mr Bere. The next day, Mr Bere wrote his *short impudent letter* to inform Hannah that, owing to Young's recent insinuation about his moral character, he did not *consider him a fit person to instruct the youth, or lesson the aged,* of Blagdon; furthermore, although he was unwilling to start a legal enquiry, if Young continued in his present character *with the intent to render* [Bere's] *ministration in the Church as little effectual as possible,* [Bere would] *be driven to seek* [his] *remedy, where, and how* [he could].

Hannah, convinced there must have been some misunderstanding, asked Bere to send her the affidavit and suggested that Sir Abraham Elton should investigate the affair with his *usual judgement and impartiality.* Sir Abraham Elton, Baronet, had inherited Clevedon Court Estate in 1790 and was the first of his family to be securely established in the landed gentry. The Eltons had risen from very humble origins to become leading Bristol merchants, and Sir Abraham was an ordained, although no longer practising, clergyman and a fellow magistrate of Mr Bere. But he was also a friend of the More sisters and, like them, an Evangelical Anglican. "His evangelical fervour never abated, though he was not one to examine his conscience on matters of pleasure". "He had discarded his clerical garb and dressed himself" and his pretty wife, Eliza, "in the finest clothes" and, during the bitterly cold winter and spring of 1794-5, while his tenants and labourers suffered from hunger and the sheep died in the fields, they had enjoyed fashionable life on the continent. Their tour of Brandenburg-Prussia culminated in a royal wedding and a series of fetes and balls lasting until March.[16]

Patty wrote in her journal that Elton was *too fair, and his manners too much of a gentleman, for Mr Bere to settle business of conscience with. He would never meet him, but avoided even the monthly intercourse at Langford,*[17] *when they met as magistrates.*[18] But perhaps Mr Bere knew a different side of Sir Abraham, whose extreme politeness and candour "hardly concealed an autocratic will, a disposition to meddle, and an implacable determination to eradicate sin". The vicar of St Andrew's Church, Clevedon, was "incessantly haunted in his duties by the squire [Sir Abraham], who often pre-empted the pulpit and thundered out a sermon".[19] Hannah and Patty invited him to preach at their school feast days on Mendip and Sir Abraham was "flattered by the respect shown to his talents and rank in society".[19]

REV. SIR ABRAHAM ELTON, 5th Bt (1755-1842), Sir Martin Archer Shee,
Clevedon Court, The Elton Collection (The National Trust), ©NTPL/John Hammond

When the sisters returned to Cowslip Green in the spring of 1800 they found that Mr Bere had *inflamed the whole neighbourhood against their plans and proceedings, alleging that all was fanaticism and the height of enthusiasm* and threatening them with penal statutes. Mr Bere was right to mistrust Sir Abraham, who then preached a sermon to a large audience, including twelve clergymen, defending the sisters' cause and explaining what provision the law made *against clergymen of the Church of England who openly deny the Trinity.*[18]

Many letters passed on the Blagdon business[20]

Meanwhile, Mr Bere wrote to Dr Crossman that the Sunday school had degenerated under Henry Young, who had assumed *the privileges of a Licensed Conventicle*[21] [with the addition of a] *private weekly confessional*. He described how Young talked for an hour at the school *after the morning service in St Andrew's;* after the evening service there were prayers and singing and *reading a sermon;* on Monday night he held *his confessional … The smith's wife and a poor brain-shook old woman, being I understand the cracks of the school;* on Thursday night there were *prayers and singing and holding forth again*. Mr Bere did not think that *these gentle breezes of the man of war* would cause a great defection from St Andrew's, but he would not be answerable for the peace of the parish when Young *came to explode in the Tornedo of enthusiasm*. Bere was concerned that Young's practices resembled Methodism, as Mr Leeves' parish at Wrington had been *deluged with this new religion* and there was *confusion, and every evil at work*.[22]

Dr Crossman, thinking that Young had only children in his care, suggested that Mr Bere should *gently admonish him* and, if this failed, he should point out to Hannah More *the mischief that* [was] *likely to follow from* [Young's] *ignorance and fanatic spirit*. If this also failed, Bere, being a magistrate, should deal with Young as an unlicensed preacher and the occupier of the house as the holder of a private conventicle.[21] In May Mr Bere sent Silas Derrick's affidavit to Hannah and told her that he *would most cheerfully submit to the arbitration of our common friend, Sir Abraham Elton,* [if there was] *anything of a dubious nature* in the affair, but he claimed that his accusation against Young was based on solid facts. He told Hannah that he did not want to hold a public investigation into Young's conduct, but he could not prevent others from doing so, as Young was *surrounded by penal statutes* [concerning unlicensed conventicles]. He later claimed that Hannah didn't answer his letter, other than to say she was unwell, and that she never visited the Parsonage again.

In July Dr Crossman complained to Mr Bere that he had not answered his letters and had ignored his invitation to visit West Monkton during the school holidays. He hoped that Mr and Mrs Bere would visit them to discuss the problem of Mr Young. In his reply Bere told Crossman of the *abominable falsehoods,* circulated by a *religious sect* [meaning Hannah's Evangelicals]: *God knows, my dear Sir, what you have heard … It is here reported that you have written to Mrs H More, a very encouraging letter, desiring her to continue the school and acknowledging the great good it was productive of in your parish*. He asked Crossman for *a fair impartial hearing, face to face with* [his] *adversaries*, and the chance to defend his character *by appealing to the public*.

Meanwhile, Hannah, without notifying Bere or Crossman, sent a series of accusations against Mr Bere to the Bishop of Bath and Wells, probably including the charge of

Socinianism.[6] Bishop Moss was in his 80s and unable to cope with the administration of his diocese, which he left to his son, the diocesan chancellor, another Dr Moss, who sent Hannah's accusations to Dr Crossman. Crossman defended his curate but Hannah refused to let Bere have copies of the accusations, so that he could defend himself. Bere therefore wrote to Crossman and explained that the only point at issue was against the teacher: *I love Sunday Schools,* he protested, *but it does not necessarily follow, that therefore I must support unlicensed conventicles … This man is, he tells us, a Calvinist and apparently of the most firey and obstinate cast.* Bere also believed that Young held opinions which might be *disgraceful to the Church and dangerous to the state* and that, if Young was removed, he would support Mrs More. Dr Crossman then asked Hannah whether she should dismiss Young and Sir Abraham replied, on her behalf, expressing his high opinion of Young's religious and moral character. Sir Abraham then sent for Mr Young, told him of Bere's charges against him, and asked Young to make an affidavit. Hannah later regretted that she did not dismiss Young at this point but she felt herself bound to defend an innocent man.[23] Had she dismissed him there would have been no Blagdon Controversy.

Mr Bere gathered his evidence[24]

In September Dr Crossman sent all the relevant papers, including a *narrative* which Bere had been writing since the autumn of 1798, to the bishop and chancellor. He also asked the chancellor to act as arbitrator, as Hannah considered the rector to be prejudiced in Bere's favour. Crossman then asked Mr Bere to obtain affidavits of every charge which he had made against Young, especially *affidavits respecting the conduct of Young at Nailsea, and of him declaring himself a Calvinist,* which Hannah claimed he had never done. Mr Bere replied that Young had been introduced to Blagdon under Hannah More's patronage, even though his behaviour at Nailsea had been *highly reprehensible,* and he thought it very strange that Sir Abraham had heard nothing about Young's conduct at Nailsea, when he lived only two miles away. The Youngs had originally come from Bath and were *well recommended for their zeal and industry*[25] but, despite their Methodist sympathies and their quarrel with the Nailsea farmers, Hannah had moved them to Blagdon.

Meanwhile Mr Bere collected his affidavits and Hannah complained to Wilberforce: *Among Bere's affidavits, which are "as plenty as blackberries", one is taken by a lunatic, whom as such I have helped to maintain. People start up out of ditches, or from under hedges, to listen to the talk of poor pious labourers as they are at work, and then go and make an oath.*[26] But, much to the delight of Dr Crossman, Mrs Parsons, wife of a yeoman farmer who farmed his own estate in Blagdon and was then Lord of the Manor, *came forward … to state the conversation that passed between her and Young.* Crossman then sent the affidavits to Dr Moss, who instructed Hannah to dismiss Henry Young. Everything seemed to be going in the curate's favour and Hannah felt close to despair as she walked in her garden at Cowslip Green and looked at *the steeple* [tower] *and the village of Blagdon.*[26] But she refused to dismiss Young and rallied Sir Abraham, who asked Mr Bere to name a day for Young to *face his accusers* at the Langford Inn. Sir Abraham decided to attend the meeting himself, as he had heard *suspicions ... respecting the credibility and competency of the said accusers* and wanted to be sure that they were false.

Mr Bere was naturally put out by this development, having understood that the bishop had already decided to dismiss Mr Young. But Dr Moss claimed that he had only given his opinion as a private person and that the matter was *clearly open to fresh investigation.* Mr Bere promptly refused to attend any meeting but Dr Crossman, who at this stage firmly supported his curate, advised him *not to shrink from it, but boldly to come forward, with* [his] *evidences in* [his] *hand,* and the chancellor agreed with him. Mr Bere was still not very happy, as Sir Abraham *was decidedly a partisan of Mrs More's cause,* so he came up with a wily solution: he told Sir Abraham that *it would not injure the cause to have many respectable judges* at the meeting and wrote to fellow magistrates and orthodox clergy, who were likely to sympathise with him. Mr Bere then took to his bed, as he was afflicted with gout, and told Sir Abraham that he was *too weak to meet* [him] *at Langford.* He suggested that the George Inn at Blagdon would be more convenient for himself and the witnesses – ensuring that all his Blagdon witnesses were able to attend – and Sir Abraham suggested that they meet at the George at 12 o'clock on 12th November.

On 3rd November Mr Bere began to write to *the most respectable gentlemen* in the neighbourhood, explaining how he had made it his duty, as curate of the parish, to inform Hannah More of the *extravagant irregularities* of her school teacher and that *this lady wrote (without* [his] *knowledge) to the Chancellor and Dr Crossman, apparently with intention to strangle the investigation, by destroying in the minds of these gentlemen, whatever respects they might have entertained of* [his] *moral and clerical character.* He invited these gentlemen to the George at 11 o'clock, to hear the witnesses resworn and to suppress *the indecent clamour* against the dismissal of Henry Young. It was obvious that Mr Bere planned to have the whole proceeding over before Sir Abraham arrived at 12 o'clock, as one of these invitations has survived, and to it Mr Bere had added a postscript: *I hope to have the pleasure of your company to dinner – the business, I apprehend, will not require one hour's attention.*[27] Unfortunately for Mr Bere, Sir Abraham must have got wind of his deceit, as the very next day he wrote to Bere and asked whether he had any objection to the meeting's being brought forward to 11 o'clock.

Patty wrote in her journal that Sir Abraham *with much difficulty ... procured from Dr Moss the thirteen affidavits obtained by Bere from different low people in his parish, in order to incriminate poor Younge. These affidavits were as wicked as they were contemptible, as they were from people of the lowest situation and worst character.*[28] Her journal ends abruptly before the meeting at the George. Hannah wrote to Wilberforce that the affidavits were *such trash … How a man of Moss's sense and knowledge of the world can lend himself to such a business is inconceivable, but … the high Church spirit must protect its own.*[29] Patty wrote to Wilberforce: *We shall have but an unfair Jury, in people who think one extempore prayer a greater evil than breaking the ten commandments.*[30]

The mock trial at the George Inn on 12th November 1800[31]

The meeting took place at the George Inn, Blagdon, [now George House, opposite The Stores] and the proceedings were documented by Mr Bere in his narrative: *There appeared for Mrs More, the Reverend Sir Abraham Elton, his attorney, Mr Fisher, Captain Simmons and Mr Descury. For Mr Bere, himself only. These gentlemen attended to rehear the cause and judge of the competency of the witnesses, upon whose testimony Dr Moss, as arbitrator, had before determined it: Francis Edwards Whalley Esq was in the chair; Samuel Baker Esq – magistrate; John Savery Esq – magistrate; Rev. Mr Blomberg, Prebend of Bristol and a magistrate; Dr Blomberg, Vicar of Banwell and Shepton Mallet; Rev. S T Wylde, Vicar of Burrington and a magistrate; Rev. Mr Barter, Rector of Timsbury; Rev. Mr Hawes, Vicar of Yatton; Major Corbet; Thomas Warren Esq; Mr Inman; Rev. Mr Leeves, Rector of Wrington.* Francis Whalley was Colonel of the 2nd Somerset Militia, lived at Winscombe Court, and was known to dislike Evangelicalism, which he equated with Methodism. All these gentlemen would undoubtedly favour Mr Bere rather than Henry Young.[32]

The thirteen witnesses appearing for Mr Bere were resworn and the seven witnesses appearing for Hannah More were sworn in. Sir Abraham Elton named himself as Hannah More's advocate and reminded those present that it was *not a court which could deal with perjury* [swearing to false evidence], *nor could anyone be called to account for what they said there.* As the whole proceeding was couched in legal language, they might be forgiven for forgetting this fact.

The affidavit of the schoolmaster, Henry Young, sworn before Sir Abraham Elton:

> *Who on his oath saith, that to the best of his knowledge, he has never avowed himself a Calvinist, nor did he ever encourage Methodist preachers, directly or indirectly. He saith also, that he is unconscious of having ever insulted the resident minister of Blagdon; but on the contrary, has strived to conduct himself towards him with all due respect. It has also been his constant endeavour to inculcate on those who frequent the schools under his direction, the propriety and necessity of paying due respect to the minister of the parish, and of being constant in their attendance on the service of the church.*

The deposition of Mary Clark, wife of Ambrose Clark of Blagdon, sworn before Thomas Bere:

Who on her oath deposeth that her husband and James Filer were talking in her husband's orchard with Henry Young … That she then and there, in the presence of her husband and James Filer, heard the said Henry Young declare, that he was a Calvinist.

The George Inn, Blagdon
(George Symes collection, BLHS Archives)

The deposition of James Filer, house-keeper of Blagdon, sworn before Thomas Bere:

Who on his oath deposeth that once having a conversation with Henry Young … on religious subjects, he asked the said Henry Young what principles he was of; Henry Young answered and said, he was a Calvinist. [Ambrose Clark and Margaret Thorne also swore that they had heard Young declare himself a Calvinist.]

The information of Betty Emery, aged 77, of Blagdon, sworn before Thomas Bere:

Who on her oath deposeth that one – Veal, a person who is generally reputed a Methodist teacher, some time since requested to leave his horse at her door, for that he was going on down to Mr Henry Young … He had heard he (Mr Young) was a good man and he asked this deponent if she attended his school? She said she used to go, but had left off going for some time; he further said that he had been sent for to go to visit a woman in the parish of Blagdon; and this deponent ... has heard, that ... Mr Veal was to visit Molly Spiring, one of Mr Young's chief disciples.

The deposition of Thomas Huish, house-holder in Blagdon, sworn before Thomas Bere:

Who on his oath saith that one John Baker senior, one of Mr Henry Young's private scholars, one day endeavouring much to persuade this deponent to become a member of their society, said that Mr Young saved souls, but that Mr Bere did not try to save them. This deponent further saith that ... John Baker told him that he had been for a week to Bristol to hear the Methodists and liked them desperate; and he saith he should go again very soon, and that he never heard such preaching in his life, and moreover that Mr Young could explain the scriptures better than Mr Bere, a thousand times better.

The deposition of Thomas Bere, clerk, sworn before S. T. Wylde, Vicar of Burrington:

This deponent on his oath saith that having visited, as a minister, a poor sick woman of the name of Sarah Dirrick (since dead) who had attended Young's school formerly, but latterly had not. She, Sarah Dirrick, (then near death) declared ... that she heard the following conversation between one Dennis Stallard, a Methodist teacher, and Molly Spiring, one of Mr Young's most constant private scholars. Stallard asked Spiring if she knew the meaning of this scripture, "that false teachers should arise and should deceive, if it were possible, the elect"? They both agreed that the church ministers were the false teachers. She also added that another Methodist teacher used to come to Molly Spiring's and she had seen him there at prayers with her.

The declaration of Sarah Dirrick, house-keeper in Blagdon, sworn before Thomas Bere:

Who on her oath saith that she had a conversation with one Hannah Needs, one of Mr Young's private scholars, who told this deponent that, if this deponent entered into his society, she must make extempore prayer, or she could not be admitted. This deponent went and heard one Joseph White, a taylor, Thomas Baker and John Baker, labourers, all these Mrs More's underteachers, make long extempore prayer but this deponent did not so pray. She also heard Molly Spiring pray extempore in the private school. This deponent further says that she left off going to school and, afterwards, going up to the parsonage (one Sunday evening), where her son was in service, to hear Mr Bere read the scriptures to his family, which is his constant practice to do, she met Molly Spiring and Nancy Leman going to Mr Young's school. Molly Spiring said, "where are you going"?

Deponent answered, "to Mr Bere's". "I doubt you are going the wrong way", said Molly Spring. Deponent answered, "I hope not", and then left her. This deponent further saith that she was sent for to come in and see a poor sick neighbour and found her very considerably troubled in her mind. Molly Smith, the sick woman, told this deponent that Henry Young … came to see her and pray to her but, when he went away, he told the sick woman, "Well, I cannot promise that you will be saved, for you have not got faith enough".

The information of Sarah, the wife of the Rev. Thomas Bere, being the account of her visit to Young's Monday evening school, sent in a letter to Hannah in January 1799, with the following addition:

[Henry Young began by] *relating to his audience the great persecutions he had suffered ever since he had been walking in the ways of the Lord, which he said was about fourteen years, and that all those who would walk in the ways of the Lord, must expect to meet with persecutions; but the Lord, he said, brought good out of evil; for had it not been for the persecutions he had met with at Nailsea, he should not have been there to teach them now, and they might have been still in their ignorance;* [Young then referred to a book he had lent to one of the men which described] *three Christians dresses: one white, one red and one black; and said it would be a glorious time when they had attained the white one.* [When Young examined the people individually], *asking how they found themselves?* [they all replied] *that their desire was to walk in the ways of the Lord* [but that] *they found great trials. One of them complained of having been in great darkness, but … was quite comfortable now;* [another told Mr Young] *that one morning he forgot to say his prayers, until going to his work, at a certain stile, he recollected that he had not said his prayers, and there he kneeled down and said them.* [Mr Young then asked his wife the same question] *and her reply was very similar.* [On another occasion Mrs Bere had called at the house of one of the private scholars, Molly Spring, who had told her] *that when she first began to seek the Lord, she was very much troubled in her mind, and that she prayed earnestly to the Lord and that she was in the agony, and then she came all over in a sweat, and that then she knew she was in the birth, and she felt the Holy Ghost come into her, and she was then so light, she could have flown through the window.*

The deposition of Margaret Thorne, wife of Thomas Thorne, carpenter, of Blagdon, sworn before Thomas Bere:

[Margaret stated that she had been] *bred in the church and confirmed by the bishop* [but had also been a] *constant attendant on the public schools of Henry Young,* [who told her that he would be pleased to see her and Thomas at his private school. Margaret asked Young what his religion was and he replied], *I am a Calvinist.* [She attended the first of Young's private schools with about twelve others. The meeting opened] *with a long extempore prayer by Young, in which he prayed for the French, then suffering for righteousness sake.*[33] [Then he asked] *Joseph White, a taylor to pray extempore, which White did in many words.* [Next he asked] *Paul Bush, a pauper, and he prayed extempore* [and then everyone present was asked to do the same. Margaret said to Young], "*Sir, I am not used to extempore prayer*", *and she refused.* [Margaret then explained how Young had asked the men and then the women, individually], *in what state they found their souls?* [When he asked Margaret, she replied that she didn't see any reason for confessing her sins to Young, but preferred to pray to God in secret. Margaret claimed that he laughed scornfully at her and told her]:

"*You should do as I have done – I have been wicked myself … I myself, as Jacob did, wrestled with angels eight and forty hours, scarcely breaking my fast, taking but just something to keep me alive, and then I became converted*"… *He then individually asked the women of their estate, … one of them (Molly Spring) said, "a stranger asked of her the road to the hill, (Mendip) she said, she thought he was a stranger in the land and she ought to be kind to him; she then prayed to her great Jehovah, that she might direct him in the way, and she found it was right so to do". Young said, Now Mrs Spring, as I said before, we ought to be kind to strangers; here's wars and fightings; one nation against another,*[33] *as one neighbour against another; ought not we to be kind to these strangers, our enemies, as they call them! Certainly, Sir, said Mrs Spring … In the course of the meeting, this Molly Spring, and the blacksmith's wife* [Sexy Baber, wife of Hellier Baber], *and Young's wife, made pretty long extempore prayers. Young closed the meeting with a long extempore prayer, an hymn was then sung, and the meeting broke up.* [On another occasion Margaret Thorne had been talking to Henry Young in his house on religious subjects when Young said], "*The church service in the prayer book was very good to some people to be sure, but it did not in his opinion agree with the scripture; for it was a form of prayer for the ministers". This deponent coming from church, one Sunday, spoke to the blacksmith's wife, and praised the sermon they had heard …* [Mrs Baber] *laughed and said she thought so much of Mr Young, that Mr Bere did her but very little good!* [Margaret replied] "*Why should you go to hear Mr Bere at all?*" [Mrs Baber] *said she liked to hear Mr Load, the Curate of Ubley, for he was a dear good man. "If you want to save your soul, you must go to Mr Young or Mr Load".* [Bere later noted that Mr Load was] *generally considered to be of a particular way of thinking,* [meaning that he was, like Hannah, an Evangelical Anglican.]

The next evidence against Young was a letter from Mary Parsons, Lady of the Manor, to Mrs Bere. Mr and Mrs Parsons lived at Blagdon Court but this letter was written on October 12th 1800 at Mount Beacon, their winter home in Bath, in response to questions sent to her by Mrs Bere. It was subsequently verified on oath in front of J. Slade, magistrate:

I remember perfectly well to have called on Mr Young on the morning when last at your house. I told him, I thought he treated you very coolly, and that you felt yourself hurt at his behaviour; and that if it proceeded from the letter you wrote Mrs H More, he was wrong, as it was at her request you visited the school; and gave her every information. I told him he might see a copy of the letter: He said he did not care for the letter, or for any man and that there was nothing done in that school, but what Mrs More knew and approved of; and that he thought he had done some good there; and that he would stay there as long as it pleased the Lord, or that he could do good, and when that failed, he would leave the place and go where he could do good, for he thought it his duty to preach the word of God, and that he should like to go a missionary abroad, as he thought he could do more good there; otherwise, he would follow his own trade as a shoemaker, as it would be more beneficial to his family. These are his own words, as near as I can recollect … I am certain that I have frequently heard H Young, and likewise the Mores say, that it was not their desire to establish a school merely for children, and that it should not be made a nursery of, and that it was intended to instruct the grown up. You ask me, if I recollect Mrs Martha More recommending a sermon? – I certainly do – She said it was a very excellent one. It was not written by one of the Church of England, but that she did not regard. These are the words as near as I can recollect … During our residence in the parish, for thirteen years … I think there can be but one opinion of Mr Bere - that as a clergyman, a magistrate, or a private gentleman, he has done his duty as far as lay in his power.

The deposition of Ann Stephens, sworn before Thomas Bere magistrate:

Who on her oath deposeth that being in church the Sunday before Easter last, when Mr Bere, the minister, was reading the exhortation to the blessed sacrament, and was speaking these words: "Therefore, if there be any of you who by this means cannot quiet his own conscience herein, but requireth further comfort or counsel, let him come to me, etc". Mrs Young, wife of Henry Young, … touched Betty Baker, one of the underteacher's wives, with her elbow, and lifted up her eyes with evident marks of scorn and contempt.

The deposition of John Box Esq, sworn before Thomas Bere, magistrate: [John Box had evidently been sent by Mr Bere to enquire about Henry Young's reputation in Nailsea, where he had been Hannah's school master before Blagdon.]

Mr Box called at the house of Mr Coombes who told him that he knew Young *but did not like to speak anything against him: but on being requested to declare what he knew, Mr Coombes said, Young, when in their parish, attended the children of his school to meet Mrs More at a feast given by her on Mendip to her schools; that he and a neighbouring farmer overtook Young and his school returning from the feast, and found Young "very, very much in liquor"; that he remonstrated with Young, as being unfit to take care of the children; upon which*

Young challenged him to fight with sword and pistol; this he declined, and he and others, took away their children from the school. NB Young came to the parish [Vestry Meeting] *and offered to go on his knees, if Mr Coombes would forgive him. Mr Coombes said, he forgave him, but never sent his children afterwards. Notwithstanding Young was continued Mrs H More's schoolmaster at Nailsea, till he was removed to Blagdon.*

The declaration of Richard Derrick of Blagdon, sworn in front of Thomas Bere, magistrate:

Who on his oath declareth that some time past, being in the company of John Baker junior, of Blagdon aforesaid, he heard the said John Baker say that Mrs Hannah More informed Joseph White of Blagdon, taylor, on seeing him at Cheddar club, "that there would be great alteration in the parish of Blagdon within a short time". Whereupon said deponent (wishing to know what alteration was to be made) was told by said John Baker, that it was verily believed and almost certain that the Rev. Mr Bere would not be suffered to preach in the parish of Blagdon much longer. John Baker, laborer [sic] and Joseph White, taylor, are teachers in Mrs More's school at Blagdon.

The following witnesses appeared for Hannah More and Henry Young:

James Tucker, shoemaker, once an inmate, and now a disciple of Young
Joseph White, taylor and under teacher, member of the private meeting
John Baker, labourer and under teacher, member of the private meeting
Paul Bush, a pauper, under teacher, member of the private meeting
Betty Baker, a teacher's wife, member of the private meeting
John Baker, a teacher's father, member of the private meeting
Sexy Baber, the blacksmith's wife, member of the private meeting

Mr Bere later noted that *the depositions of these persons seemed so little relevant, so confused, and of such a questionable nature, that no one I believe took down their evidence.* At least, this is what he hoped the public would believe. He also claimed that Hannah's witnesses had been bribed. At no point was Mr Young called to answer his accusers.

After every possible exertion of Sir A Elton, whose heart indubitably was in the cause, wrote Mr Bere, *the examination closed, and I withdrew, expecting that those who were interested would follow my example, in this I was mistaken. I was very soon requested to come forward, when the chairman, in manner and in words I shall never forget, informed me of the gentlemen's judgement.* Not surprisingly the judgement was in Bere's favour and he later noted: *After the repeated repulses of my adversaries, thus honourably and immaculately restored to my station in society, I ejaculated in my usual voice, Thank God, the church has succeeded.*

The aftermath of the meeting[34]

That evening, the meeting at the George having concluded in his favour, Mr Bere took several of the *most respectable gentlemen* back to the parsonage for dinner; the bell-ringers were paid to ring the church bells; and several houses in the village, including the parsonage, were illuminated with candles. The next day Colonel Whalley wrote to Mr Bere:

> *I shall with great pleasure give you the opinion or judgement of the gentlemen yesterday at Blagdon; and I must observe it was unanimous, ... "That you had done away every imputation on your character; that the schoolmaster had behaved extremely improper; that at all events the private school ought to be abolished; and that he ought not to be continued at all as a schoolmaster at Blagdon without your approbation." As Chairman, I did not give my opinion formally, ... but I sufficiently expressed myself, to several gentlemen present, as being of the same opinion; had I formally given in my vote, I should have added, that I thought Mr Bere very injuriously treated.*

Apparently convinced of the truth of the evidence against Young, Colonel Whalley was pleased at the outcome of the meeting, which *dealt a blow to the increase of evangelical religion, which he, with the great majority of the laity and ... of the clergy also, called Methodism.* Despite his views on religion, Colonel Whalley was a kind man and respected by the More sisters, although he disliked them.[35] Richard Whalley, his youngest brother, was an Evangelical clergyman, whom the sisters invited to their Sunday School anniversary feasts and who described his brother Francis as a *decided enemy of all serious* [Evangelical] *religion.*[36]

Mr Bere received a very different letter from Sir Abraham: *I shall take the liberty to observe, with all due respect to the gentlemen you was pleased to convene on the occasion, that they went beyond their power, in proceeding with so much ceremony to something like a final sentence upon Young. ... Mrs Hannah More cannot possibly acknowledge **their jurisdiction**; and ... should her school in the parish be immediately put an end to (and I shall beyond all doubt advise the measure) it will not be in consequence of any thing which occurred yesterday.* He added that the credibility of the depositions against Young was questionable owing to the *contradictions on the opposite side, although the gentlemen who assumed the office of judges thought proper to pay so little attention to them* [and, as they were not written down, he could not form an opinion]. He also felt that Mrs Parsons' affidavit had been *produced unfairly* [and] *no time had been allowed for the persons implicated to put in their answers to it.* Finally Sir Abraham told Bere that, although there was nothing against Bere's *conduct as a man in procuring the depositions* [in his opinion Bere had] *acted wrong as a magistrate in taking them* [himself.]

The closure of the Blagdon School[37]

Meanwhile Hannah had found a new champion in Dr Thomas Sedgwick Whalley, the second of the three Whalley brothers, to whom she wrote: *Bere is triumphant! It is said he has received a letter from Wells, thanking him for his zeal in defence of the Church, and ordering Young to be dismissed.*[38] Rather than dismiss Young, whom she still supported, Hannah closed her Blagdon school on 16th November, as she always maintained that she would not run a school without the support of the parish clergyman.

Dr Crossman was concerned that the school, which Hannah thought *so beneficial to the interests of the people,* was to be closed *merely because the present teacher was deemed unfit to superintend the instruction of the children* [in] *his charge.* Mr Bere therefore offered to open a similar school, under his own direction, *for the establishment of which* [he] *had offered, to the Rector, a subscription of five guineas annually out of his stipend. The affluent Rector,* Mr Bere later noted, *did not offer to be sure one farthing for this purpose; but he had the goodness to observe, in a very serious manner, that the sum the curate tendered was very little.* Bere was also annoyed that the rector still thought the school was only for children, as Hannah More herself had said that *it was not their design to establish a school merely for children; it should not be made a nursery of - it was intended to instruct the grown-up.* [Mr Bere was also mistaken, but it suited his purpose.] *In other words,* he wrote, *to lessen the labour of the Curate, by taking the spiritual guidance of his flock out of his charge, delivering it into the hands of Henry Young, Mrs More's teacher. One who thinks it his duty to preach the word of God, who has preached unordained, and would like to go a missionary.*

Blagdon had lost much more than the Sunday school, as Hannah told Dr Whalley, *the poor people of Blagdon meet together to deprecate the cruelty which has robbed them of so many blessings, especially the clothing and school of industry; but they say they dare not speak out, lest the Justice should send them to Shepton* [gaol].[39] The sisters had provided clothing for the poor children, and the school of industry had taught the older girls and women how to sew, spin wool and knit stockings which could be sold to give them an income.

Thomas Sedgwick Whalley and Mendip Lodge[40]

Dr Whalley, like Elton and Crossman, was an absentee clergyman, who left his Lincolnshire benefice in the charge of a curate but, unlike Elton, he was not an Evangelical, which made him a more valuable ally. In 1774, on his marriage to Elizabeth Sherwood, the widow of John Jones Esq of Langford, Dr Whalley had come into the possession of a large fortune and an estate at Langford Court, now the home of the Wills family. Soon after, he bought the centre house in the newly built Royal Crescent at Bath so that they could spend their winters in the city. In 1783 they had closed down both houses and spent several years on a tour of France, Italy and Belgium, returning to England in the summer of 1787. As Langford Court had been let to Mr Hiley Addington, Dr Whalley *commenced building a cottage on the lofty hill of the Mendip range, which … was added to from time to time till it grew into a mansion.*

Mendip Lodge

Dr Whalley covered *the mountainous site on which it was erected … with firs and deciduous trees* [and] *thousands of acres* [of trees] *which now adorn* [Mendip] *owe their origin to this beginning. In this delightful summer residence Dr Whalley spent several months for many years.* [The Whalleys] *were fond of Doleberry Warren (a part of his estate, which abounded with rabbits).* The summer residence was originally called Langford Cottage but as it grew into a large fashionable residence, the name was changed to Mendip Lodge. The house, now demolished, was situated on the hills opposite the present site of Pear Tree Garage at Upper Langford, so the Whalleys were relatively close neighbours of the More sisters, who had moved to Cowslip Green in 1785.

The emissaries of Satan and the Bishops[41]

Soon after the meeting at the George Inn, Patty received *a most ambiguous and alarming note* from Beilby Porteus, the Bishop of London, *expressing utmost terror on* [Hannah's] *account, yet refusing to explain himself … What out of tenderness he seems to have concealed*, wrote Hannah to Wilberforce, *is, that this mock trial has been fabricated by Bere's emissaries into an official one, and that I am found guilty of sedition and, perhaps, taken up and sent to prison.*[42] Patty asked Dr Whalley if he would visit them at Cowslip Green, as *such horrid reports are abroad, that some strong measures must be taken and immediately. The emissaries of Satan are spreading strange things in London; even the Bishop writes in great agitation and alarm, as if dreadful things have reached his ears. We have sent for Sir Abraham Elton to meet you, it being of great importance it should be before the Langford meeting.*[17] *My sister Hannah is again ill, we are alarmed about her. This affair, I fear will destroy her.*

Mr Bere and his *emissaries* had been busy writing to bishops, *chiefly to those most attached to* Hannah. But she too had been busy writing to the bishops, many of whom were her friends. Porteus and the aristocratic Barrington, Bishop of Durham, had been Hannah's friends since her London days and there is little doubt that they used their influence to support her. Barrington had even *set up several little readings in* [the sisters'] *manner.* Hannah also wrote to Pretyman, the High Church Bishop of Lincoln, who disliked *enthusiasm* [but was] *an avowed patron of private instruction of the poor.* He had also subscribed to her *Cheap Repository Tracts* and offered Hannah warm support, acquitting her of *enthusiasm.*[43]

The plotting at Cowslip Green[44]

Although Hannah had resolved not to defend herself, she now became busy behind the scenes, directing the efforts of both Sir Abraham and Dr Whalley. This was duplicitous but the subterfuge was forced on her by gender conventions that damned a woman if she kept silent and damned her still more if she defended herself.[45] Hannah's letters to Whalley reveal in detail the plotting which went on at Cowslip Green. It seems strange today that they corresponded by letter when they lived so close to each other, but this was before the telephone and an immediate reply was possible if they sent a servant on horseback or even on foot.

In the autumn of 1800 Dr Whalley wrote an extremely long letter to Dr Moss, which the sisters had been copying for him: *My poor sister Betty has been ill in bed above a week,* wrote Hannah, *but the others are copying away, and we hope at least to secure all the prominent parts and striking passages … This letter, this volume rather, is indeed a labour of love.* However there were *one or two slight matters in which a trivial mistake was made,* which Hannah *erased.* Whalley had also been writing letters to the local clergy on Hannah's behalf, in which his *views of truth and justice* had led him to criticise his older brother, Francis. Much to Hannah's delight, Dr Whalley had managed to persuade some of the clergy and his brother, Francis, to change their opinion of the Blagdon school and its master. *I never thought,* wrote Hannah, *of you or your brother, much less of any other clergyman, signing this recantation of the partie quarree; but, besides their statement to the Chancellor and your letter, I had an idea of a third plan ... for the public, particularly such men as* [the High Church clergyman Charles] *Daubeny, who having already attacked me, and being the intimate friend of Barter, I have little doubt they will get me into some reviews or papers.* Her idea was that the local clergy who supported her might subscribe to a paper, to be written by Dr Whalley, relating how she *had been so atrociously treated by a neighbouring curate as to compel* [her] *to give up the school (though earnestly requested to continue it by the rector, even after this mock trial)* and how they were afraid she might relinquish her other schools, which had benefited morals and *helped to fill churches.* Hannah told Whalley that *Three persons, of the best credit in Blagdon, have offered to swear that two of Bere's witnesses have repeatedly declared that they were sent for* [whereas Bere claimed that they were volunteers]. *Another most kind letter from the Bishop of London, in which he tells me, though with deep abhorrence of the author, that sedition is the cry against me in London.*

When the Bere *partie* heard that their friends had changed sides, there were scenes of great mirth at Cowslip Green. *Oh! that I could be present to see the oyster at Wrington* [Mr Leeves] *made broad awake, struggling to get out of his shell, and driven back again by its native frigidity,* wrote Patty to Whalley. *Did you hear us laugh and scream at reading your more than incomparable letter?* Only four other local clergymen now remained in the *clerical partie quarree,* as Patty called them: Lewes, Blomberg, Hawes and Wylde. *Snail* [Mr Leeves?] *was here the whole morning and went away as impenetrable as he came, though whetted by my sister all the time. We find by him that the four are terribly frightened* [as] *a report is gone forth, and now prevails all over Bristol, that these four valiant defenders of the faith appeared at this celebrated court of judicature* [the George Inn] *to put down Hannah More and her schools ... Perhaps it may not be amiss to let them do something. We must keep the copy of your letter to show and enjoy it with our anti-oyster baronet* [Sir Abraham] *... Have you seen Bere's letter of invitation to the four constellations, which appears to us strongly to implicate the Chancellor?* [Chancellor Moss claimed that he knew nothing about the meeting in the George.] *Enclosed are the objections Hannah gave Leeves to the manifesto of the animated four. Am I intelligible?* This letter is typical of Patty's mischievous style.

The jangle of the church bells and the Blagdon illuminations[46]

At the end of November Mr and Mrs Bere were *cordially received* by Dr Crossman in Bath and Mr Bere understood that both the Bishop and Chancellor Moss were *perfectly satisfied* with his conduct. However, in December, while the Drs Moss were in London, they were influenced by the Bishops of London and Durham, and *a strange and unexpected alteration took place,* Bere later wrote in his narrative, *THE CAUSE OF WHICH I may conjecture, but dare not presume, to account for - The effect, however, of this resolution,* **I have very severely felt.** *It seemed meant to crush the credit of my character; it has only crippled my finances.*

The bishop, who had heard from Dr Crossman about the jubilation in Blagdon, replied that he disapproved of Bere's connivance *at the bell ringing etc, which, as a magistrate, it was his duty immediately to have stopped.* Moreover, Bere should not have said *the meeting was under Dr Moss's sanction and direction.* Mr Bere was very indignant and noted in his narrative: *Who told Dr Moss of Bere's connivance ... that the parsonage was illuminated ... and that there was exhibited a large transparency inscribed with the words "CHURCH TRIUMPHANT"? ... [Dr Moss should] have made some enquiry of the Curate before he presumed to use the unqualified expression "connivance" to a brother clergyman.* On 15th December, complaining of painful gout and feeling very sorry for himself, Mr Bere wrote to Dr Crossman:

I am even now more fit to be in my bed-chamber, than to write on this subject ... Sir, I may be permitted to say, that more than once in perilous circumstances, I have ventured my life in my magisterial capacity, for the public good, and if there had been anything more than rustic mirth, and an unfortunate attachment of the parishioners to their Curate, who had dwelt among them for more than seventeen years, I should not have been wanting, if my duty as a magistrate required my presence ... After having been standing near six hours, in a very infirm state; and all that time, seeing the **violent efforts** *made by that party* [Hannah More's] *to render me odious and infamous, when the decision took place, and I felt myself restored, I did ejaculate,* **not exclaim,** *for I spoke in my usual tone of voice ... "Thank God, the Church has succeeded" ... I knew nothing of the intention of the people to jangle the 3 bells till I heard them; I was then in a carriage going home, having Mr Savery and Major Corbet with me; I believe I expressed my disapprobation of it to those gentlemen ... I am not certain of this, or indeed many other occurrences that immediately took place. On my arrival at the parsonage, I found Mrs Bere had sent to stop the bell-ringing; the people refused and they did ring some time; or rather, they chimed: There must have been 3 persons concerned, for there were 3 bells.*[47]

There dined with me that evening, Mr Barter, Mr Savery, Major Corbet, Mr Baker, Mr Inman and Mr Warren; they heard this jangling, but it did not appear that either of these Gentlemen thought it either tumultuous or dangerous. [A neighbour called on the Beres the next day and told them that] *there were* **three cottages** *that had candles lighted: the turnpike cot, inhabited by a poor old cripple, being one ... MR BERE DID NOT GIVE A GUINEA TO THE THREE RINGERS, TO RING, but ... those people said they wondered if Mr Bere would give them anything for ringing? To this one of the neighbours replied he could not say ... but they might have five shillings worth of punch, and if Mr Bere would not pay for it, he would. The next ... evening, this person called at the parsonage and told Mrs Bere this, the parish being perfectly still, Mrs Bere gave this person half a guinea without Mr Bere's knowledge ... If Dr Moss will put any questions to me, I will answer them openly and fairly, but I will not be harassed to death by the idle suggestions of my opponents.*

More plotting at Cowslip Green: Bere's narrative and the testimonial of the four clergymen[48]

Meanwhile Mr Bere had been writing a *narrative* about *the infamous Blagdon affair* which he lent to Dr Crossman and which he intended to publish. Hannah heard about this in December when she travelled to Bath with Thomas Simmons, who lived in Wrington and now considered Bere *guilty of the most palpable falsehoods, on that extraordinary day at Blagdon*. Hannah thought it *absolutely necessary* that Dr Whalley should read it and when she learned that Mr Bere intended *to print all Dr Crossman's letters, written in the closest confidence,* she became very worried that Hiley Addington, Whalley's tenant at Langford Court, might subscribe his name to it. Mr Addington, brother of the next prime minister, had a *decided dislike for the instruction of the poor* and wouldn't listen to Hannah's friends. But he *suffered his mind to be warped by the falsehoods of his bailiff and,* Hannah told Whalley in confidence, by the *whispers and insinuations* of the Vicar of Burrington, Mr Wylde, who was angry that Hannah had managed to obtain the living of Brockley for Mr Boak, as he had hoped for it himself.

In December, the *clerical judges* – Lewes, Blomberg, Hawes and Wylde – had dined at James Simmons' house in Wrington to write a testimonial for Dr Moss. But Hannah would not consent to its being sent, unless Dr Whalley was *allowed to infuse some of* [his] *spirit into it,* and also suggested that the clergy should be sent Mr Drewitt's letter to Dr Crossman, Mrs Parsons' affidavit and her letter explaining *the offensive word "preach"* and the insinuation that Hannah's school was really for adults, not children. Mr Bere had *declared that all his deponents were volunteers* but Mrs Parsons now claimed that her evidence against Young *had been wormed out of* [her] *gradually, and then she was surprised into an oath.* [She had also told] *Patty her regret at having gone with Mrs Bere to disturb the quiet of those few poor people, who met on a Monday evening for religious conversation; she declared she saw not the least harm in it.*

Hannah told Whalley: *I wish, my dear sir, that you, and, if they were willing, the four clergymen, would see some of the best farmers in Blagdon. James Simmons tells me Farmer Young is a most respectable man; see him, pray, and his son; they attended these meetings … and both father and son can tell some things which* [the four clergy] *ought to hear before they write to the Chancellor. Woollen, the shopkeeper, also has been told by Mary Clerk* [Clark], *one of the witnesses against Young, that she was sent for* [to give evidence]; *so say several others; but Woollen is so poor, I should not like to expose him to Bere's revenge; I dare say he would own it to you. Indeed their dread of* [Mr Bere], *as a justice, makes all, except such independent men as Farmer Young, afraid to speak out.* [Chancellor Moss had denied all knowledge of the meeting at the George, but Hannah thought Bere's letters of invitation had] *said it was at the Chancellor's desire …You will make such extracts from this letter as your wisdom shall direct. Of course, you will not show it to the conclave of the*

"George", not even to Mr Leeves. My confidence in you is unbounded; but, though some people mean well, they have not capacity enough to be trusted. I hope you and Mr R Whalley will have the drawing up of the general paper of the clergy afterwards. Surely something of the belief, as to Bere's principles, should go to Dr Moss; he believes it is only my fancy. Burn this when made use of.

Meanwhile the sisters had a very obliging visit ... from Mr and Mrs Blomberg. He is full of regret at what has passed. He did not know till [his visit to James Simmons] yesterday but that Bere was the most immaculate of characters ... I am persuaded ... that you would easily induce him to write to the Chancellor ... a strong honest letter from one of the four ... might cause the scales to drop from his eyes. Leeves' letters rather thicken them.

Hannah then wrote again to Whalley [29th]: I have no right to advise anything in the present letter of the four clergy, but I think some notice should be taken of the shocking turn given to a common expression of mine. Whenever I open a school, I always say to the mothers ... and before the clergyman: "Remember, I do not go to this expense merely to take in your little brats to relieve you from the trouble of nursing them; if you will not send your big children, we shall not take your little ones; we do not keep a nursery but a school." [Hannah didn't take children under six years old.] This has been converted by Mrs Parsons' affidavit into a strong insinuation that the school was only a pretence, and that the Conventicle, as Mr Bere is pleased to call it [the Monday evening school] was the real object. As Colonel Whalley had been prejudiced against the school by Mr Bere, Hannah asked Dr Whalley to caution [his brother] not to [turn] the Wedmore and other west country farmers against the remaining schools which [were] very flourishing. Then she returned to the testimonial of the four clergy, which, she told Whalley, only goes to clear themselves and, if possible, to save Bere ... I beg you will oppose its being sent; I shall appear to owe an obligation to them ... They make no use of the information obtained by Drewitt's and Mrs Parsons' letter, in falsifying her affidavit, and ... it leaves Bere as white as it found him.

Mr Parsons[49] apparently did not share his wife's opinions, as Hannah informed Whalley: Mr Parsons and Peg have been scouring the country to get testimonies to the purity of Peg and the piety of the curate. Also that a prosecution is to be commenced against Mr Boak, at the approaching Taunton assizes, for defamation of said Peg, whom Mr Parsons declares to be one of the finest characters in the country. "Said Peg" was Margaret Thorn, one of Mr Bere's witnesses at the George, who had an illegitimate child when she was fifteen and had gone to Mr Boak as a wet nurse. Mr Boak had written to Sir Abraham to discredit her as a witness; Dr Crossman sent the letter to the Chancellor and a copy to Mr Bere, who replied: Mr Boak, Sir, is a particular friend and agent in some of her affairs for Mrs More ... and it is here understood, that Lady procured him the living of Brockley. Where was this Gentleman at the day of the trial? That was the time Boak should have confronted Margaret Thorn.[50]

Hannah More's patronage of Evangelical clergy[51]

Hannah More was one of the most influential lay people on the Mendips and she used her influence to procure livings for her young Evangelical protégés. It is likely that the cathedral clergy were reluctant to take a stand against a determined woman with a national reputation,[52] but some of the local clergy saw her lay patronage as intrusion and were, understandably, angry. When the sisters first came to Cowslip Green they found the Mendips remote and neglected by the Church. Many parishes, like Blagdon, had absentee clergy – Cheddar had only one service a week[11] – and resident clergy were poor and often neglectful, such as the clergyman who *was intoxicated about six times a week, and was very frequently prevented from preaching by black eyes, earned in fighting!* The aged Rector of Shipham *had claimed the tithes for fifty years, but had never catechised a child or preached a sermon for forty.* Hannah's solution to this problem was, by *interference and perseverance* to place *serious* [Evangelical] clergy in neglected parishes. When the Rector of Shipham died Hannah persuaded the Dean and Chapter of Wells to appoint James Jones. She also secured the curacy of Cheddar for John Boak, and when Boak was moved to Brockley he was replaced by Thomas Drewitt. Hannah also invited "her" clergy to preach at her school and club feasts and even instructed them in her theology and corrected "little errors" in their sermons. Through her schools and her *serious clergy* she aimed to convert the Mendip people to Evangelical religion. In 1798 Patty had written in her journal: *This neighbourhood, once so destitute of the gospel, is now more promising. Mr Drewitt, our curate at Cheddar, is growing into great seriousness, and already preaches extempore, and extremely well. Mr Boak has two churches very near that, and Winscombe has a very promising young man. At Axbridge, contrary to all the schemes and artful plans of the rector, there is a young man of no bad promise.*

Perhaps unwittingly, Hannah had been making enemies because of this intrusion and it was not surprising that the Bath layman Edward Spencer later called her the *She-Bishop.*[53] But a far more dangerous enemy was the High Church clergyman, Charles Daubeny, whose *Guide to the Church* was critical of Anglican Evangelical theology.

Dr Moss and Dr Crossman changed sides leaving Mr Bere very exposed[54]

At the end of the year 1800 Dr Whalley wrote to Chancellor Moss, who had read Mr Bere's narrative and had been defending *Bere's conduct, from a total ignorance of his character.* Dr Moss replied that he was *astonished and shocked at the disclosure which* [Dr Whalley's] *letter* [made] *of the duplicity, hypocrisy, and impudence of Mr Bere* [and thanked him for his] *kindness in not troubling* [his] *father ... "He has been for some time averse to business of every kind, and his feelings are easily hurt; nor do I know anything more likely to vex him than the detail of Mr Bere's conduct."*

While the More sisters were in Bath that winter, they were twice visited by Dr Crossman, who was now *a complete convert ... to the atrocity of his curate's conduct, and to the innocence ... of Young*, having been kept *completely in the dark* by the Chancellor, who had not sent him Dr Whalley's *explanatory* letter. Hannah told Crossman about Bere's heretical preaching at Axbridge, which the Chancellor did not believe. Although Hannah had not heard him herself, she said that Bere's *heretical sermon there, with a pointed denial of the Trinity, ... raised such a flame among his friends that he went again to unpreach his own doctrines, and that it was of this second sermon the Chancellor heard.* Dr Crossman told her *he could not get rid of* [Bere] *nor was he sure that even the Bishop could, without legal proof of these offences.* The rector was also shocked to hear that Bere's witnesses at the George were not volunteers. Hannah then wrote to Dr Whalley, wondering whether Bere could be *unjusticed* [for] *suborn*[ing] *witnesses for the ruin of* [Henry Young] *and* [making] *use of such deponents as Margaret Thorne ... When you and Mrs Whalley have read this letter, be so good as to burn it, for my nerves are so weak I can't bear the thought of being again brought forward.* Hannah felt that the bishop would have taken more *vigorous measures*, if he had been fit enough to be told what was going on.

The re-opening of the School[55]

In January Hannah wrote to Whalley that, after repeated requests from Dr Crossman, the school was to be reopened under Henry Young on the 25th: *My sister Patty proposes coming down to effect this restoration. She thinks of coming on Saturday to James Simmons's and to sleep there Saturday and Sunday ... How glad Patty would be to get a glimpse of you, and to thank you in all our names for the generous zeal you and Mrs W have shown throughout this whole affair ... I have implored Descury to take the most zealous pains to keep all quiet.* Mr Descury, delighted that the school was to reopen, invited Dr Whalley and Patty to dinner after morning service in Burrington, before going to the school. Mr Bere had only been ordered to leave the curacy on the 23rd and Hannah was worried that they were reopening the school in indecent haste:

> *I struggled hard to get it delayed,* [she wrote to Whalley, but] *the Wrington Methodists were eager to take advantage of the disunion between the clergyman and his parish; and as they are ever on the watch to see where they can slip in, it was to be feared that in a few days they would make their entree and perhaps attempt to draw away some of our poor people from church ... I highly approve of your reasons for not appearing at Blagdon on Sunday. I, with great earnestness, dissuaded Sir A E from his design of going. I could not bear anything like a triumph. I greatly pity these unhappy people. Patty intends to sit in a part of the church where they cannot see her. It is very painful to her to go. I have taken every precaution to prevent any outward appearance of joy in the people.*

Patty must have changed her mind as, in the event, she took the children to the church, read some prayers, and delivered a little sermon which left her audience *much affected*.[56] Whalley must also have changed his mind as Hannah later thanked him for his *generous and spirited kindness in giving* [them] *the support of* [his] *presence at the reopening of the school.* Perhaps he was tempted by the invitation to dinner at Mr Descury's before going to the school. Soon after the school was restored, Whalley became concerned that Henry Young was reading a sermon on Thursday evenings. Hannah, anxious to avoid *any fresh trouble,* ordered Young *to drop any kind of instruction but that on Sunday and at the weekly School of Industry. For the slightest disobedience, he shall,* [she assured Whalley], *be dismissed.*

The Episcopal Mandate[57]

At about this time Sir Abraham gave Bere the opportunity to clear his name by bringing *all his affidavit men* to the Langford Inn. This was also an opportunity for Young to confront his accusers and for Sir Abraham to *cross-examine them.* If this event took place, it was never mentioned by Mr Bere.[58] Meanwhile Dr Crossman wrote to Bere about the Moss's disapproval of his conduct and gave him the opportunity *of voluntarily relinquishing the curacy.* Bere replied that, although he was concerned at Dr Moss's displeasure, he could not apologise, as he did not know how he had offended. As he would not resign, the rector wrote again two days before the school reopened: *I am now commanded, by his Lordship's authority, to remove you from the Curacy of Blagdon. This letter, however, is at present a secret instrument in my possession and I shall not be forward in giving to it any degree of publicity, trusting you will preclude the necessity of such a measure, by sending me your voluntary resignation of the Curacy.* Receiving no answer to this letter, Crossman wrote again: *I fear you may have been prevented by a fit of the gout … I could wish to be favoured with a letter as soon as possible.* Mr Bere replied the following day: *Prepared as my mind was for the exultation of Mrs More's people in the certain success of their long-planned scheme to remove me, yet, I must confess that the reception of both your letters, which came together on Friday last, shocked me severely.* He thanked Crossman for keeping this to himself, but declared: *Let the MANDATE come … I would not be deprived the credit of prompt submission.*

Dr Crossman admitted to Bere that, until the meeting in the George, he had acted on his rector's advice and that, *if he had done no more and if the depositions,* [which the rector had asked for had] *been the evidences of creditable witnesses,* [then the world would still have been favourable to his cause.] *Hence I little expected to be told,* wrote Crossman, *that without my written directions you had now advanced in this ruinous controversy.* To which Mr Bere replied:

> *To convince you what character I bear at Blagdon, I have troubled Mr Parsons with a certificate, signed by the churchwardens and a great majority of the parishioners, for your*

*inspection ... **All** my parishioners of Butcombe have signed a similar testimonial.* He later noted: *The parish of Butcombe without exception have, on the experience of TWENTY YEARS borne honourable testimony to the MANNERS and MORALS and DOCTRINE of their Rector. The parish of Blagdon, with the exception of Mrs More's **very few** friends and some dependant mercenaries, have borne similar testimony on the experience of SEVENTEEN YEARS.*

Mr Bere also enclosed a copy of their agreement concerning the rectory: *... Thomas Bere shall have and hold the said rectory of Blagdon, with all rights and privileges thereunto belonging, for the tenure of ten years from 25th March 1798; paying yearly thereof two hundred and forty pounds, clear of all taxes and outgoings. Thomas Bere is to repair, and keep in repair, all the windows, tiling and thatch; Dr Crossman to rebuild and repair all the woodwork of the roofs and walls of the several buildings appertaining to the rectory. June 19th 1799.* Dr Crossman replied that the agreement between them *of course becomes void the moment that relation of Rector and Curate ceases between us.* [Bere later commented in his narrative: *Good God! Is this the reasoning of an honest man? of a Christian? of a clergyman! - I am ashamed of it.*] Crossman continued that, as Bere was not willing to leave, he had further instructions to serve him notice to quit. As his engagement began on Lady-day, Crossman asked him to finish on Lady-day, but he had no objection to Bere's staying in the parsonage house, until he was able to remove elsewhere and would remunerate him by one guinea per Sunday from Lady-day until his departure. Bere had obviously expected to be moved out of Blagdon parsonage, as he already had workmen in his Butcombe house.[59]

In February Mr Bere wrote to the bishop: *My public and private character have been, and now are, immaculate; my doctrine, and example, unexceptionable. - I therefore solicit that your Lordship will, in justice to AN OPPRESSED CLERGYMAN OF YOUR LORDSHIP'S DIOCESE, send me the ACCUSATIONS, which have so forcibly operated on your Lordship's mind, to the prejudice of my character; and also THE NAMES OF THE MALEVOLENT CALUMNIATORS; that I may be able to apply to the laws of my country for that redress which my CRUEL OPPRESSION demands.* He added that the charges brought against Margaret Thorn by Rev. Boak were *NOT FOUNDED and will be disproved - the whole is soon to undergo LEGAL INVESTIGATION.*

The chancellor replied to Mr Bere: *I am directed by father, to inform you that his instructions to Dr Crossman, to remove you from the Cure of Blagdon, were the result of very mature deliberation; and that he has not since seen any reason for thinking them too peremptory, or too precipitate.*

"Three old women in a chimney corner" and Bere's final appeal to his readers[58]

But Mr Bere was a determined man, far from defeated when he wrote the last pages of his narrative of the *Controversy*. He returned his readers to the evening of 20th January 1800 when Mr Descury and Miss David of Bristol had been guests at the parsonage and the following conversation allegedly took place:

Mr Descury having said that *he was not strictly of the Church of England and had no objection to Methodists.*
Mr Bere asked, *What may be your objection to the Church of England?*
Descury: *There are two words which I don't approve of.*
Bere: *Pray Sir, what words may these be?*
Descury: *"Three persons".*
Bere: *Indeed, Sir! What then do you think of these words in the beginning of the Book of Genesis? "And God said, let **us** make man in **our** image." There here seems to be more than one person.*
Descury: *Do you think that God sat down to consult with others, like three old women in a chimney corner, to contrive and consult how he should make the world?*
Bere: *Nothing, surely, is more commonly or plainly revealed in the New Testament than that Jesus Christ is the dearly beloved Son of God, the Father Almighty, in whom he is well pleased.*
Descury: *God the Father! I wonder then, who was God's wife?*

This was the question put by Mr D[escury], but with what intention Mr Bere did not know. But what was Mr Bere's intention when he concluded his narrative with the above conversation? Did he perhaps accuse Mr Descury of anti-Trinitarian heresy to deflect the same criticism from himself? Was he, to use Hannah's words, trying to whiten his own character by blackening Descury's? Miss David later told Hannah that *though she* [could not] *remember the words used, yet she felt herself entirely on the side of Descury, and entirely against Bere; and she adds I am a most decided Trinitarian.*[59]

Mr Bere had only told *a few particular friends* of this conversation, one of whom was Mr Edward Cross whom he met at Mr Star's in Axbridge but, nearly a year later, Descury heard that Bere had *publicly misrepresented* their conversation and had accused him of blasphemy; Bere then told Descury that he had never heard him deny the Holy Trinity and that *on no future occasion* [could he] *acknowledge* [his] *correspondence;* Crossman advised his curate to write a letter of apology, as many *characters of high repute* in Bath had great respect for Mr Descury; and Bere replied that the conversation had been *of a hypothetical nature* [and that] *the word "Trinity" was not mentioned.* Testimonials to Descury's character were sent to Dr Crossman by *Dr Maclaine, the divine, and translator of "Mosheim"*, who wrote of Descury's *patrician birth in an ancient and honourable house;* [his] *admission to the Stadtholder's Court at the Hague, where he was a favoured and useful companion of princes;* his appointment as *Captain of the Guards, in which situation his conduct and manners were untainted and exemplary;* finally *this man of the court, this captain of the guards, this worthy baron, metamorphosed into a* [Mendip] *farmer, and* [cultivated] *in this humble station the mild virtues of the honest man, the good husband, the good father, and ... a sincere and sound Christian.*[60]

Mr Bere then appealed to the only other witness to the above conversation – his wife – *whose virtuous morals and amiable manners endear her to all, whose integrity has never yet been called in question and upon whose fair fame the contaminating air of scandal has never dared to breath. Upon the present occasion it is her wish, contrary to the natural retractiveness of her character, it is her wish - for the first time in her life - under the most solemn impression of the sanctity of the appeal, to bear testimony of the expressions used by Mr Descury in the conversation alluded to.* There followed an affidavit from Mrs Bere which was an exact copy of Bere's own account.

Mr Bere ended his narrative with a final appeal to his readers:

From the unjustifiable treatment which the Curate of Blagdon has unremittingly experienced through the whole of this uncommon and, let me add, as yet, unaccountable transaction, it is indubitably manifest - THAT THERE IS SOMETHING WRONG SOMEWHERE.

If people of the description of this Henry Young are to be introduced into country parishes under one character and tolerated, perhaps encouraged, insidiously to assume another; if not children only but persons also of all ranks and ages, of divers parishes, of different characters, of various views, are to be congregated to private meetings where personal confession is used and extempore prayer made by poor, ignorant and deluded people; if all this be systematically pursued and extensively supported, let me again ask IS THERE SOMETHING WRONG SOMEWHERE?

But, if ever such things and such persons be not only countenanced, but avowedly encouraged and protected by the rulers and dignitaries of the CHURCH OF CHRIST, [ie bishops] *I may then confidently pronounce that, if in this life only they have "hope", the lowest order of the clergy in this kingdom will indeed be, of all men, the most miserable. For my part, I disdain to be querulous. "Let struck deer go weep". I have done my duty and I suffer, NOT WITHOUT PRIDE, the unjust oppression of a designing, artful and remorseless PARTY. A people who, as the admirable Quintilian says,*

"*Dum satis putant vitio carrere, in id ipsum incidunt vitium, quod virtutibus carent.*"
[While they believe that they are without fault,
their very fault is that they lack virtues.]

THE END

The Controversy became public knowledge[61]

In February 1801 Hannah wrote to Whalley: *I hear the junto* [sic] *at Blagdon are at work most sedulously on this famous narrative ... I fear* [Bere] *will stick at nothing to blacken us, and to whitewash himself.* In March Mr Bere gathered up the *famous narrative*, which presented himself as the victim, and left Bristol on the London coach, with his friend William Shaw, the Rector of Chelvey, near Nailsea, to publish a pamphlet: *The Controversy between Mrs Hannah More and the Curate of Blagdon Relative to the Conduct of her teacher of the Sunday School of that Parish with the original Letters and explanatory notes by Thomas Bere MA Rector of Butcombe near Bristol* was printed as a pamphlet and sold by booksellers in London, Bath, Bristol and Wells at the price of three shillings. Mr Bere now had the upper hand but Hannah could not help smile when she saw that his publisher, J. S. Jordan, had also published Tom Paine's *Rights of Man. - He has done our cause service,* she told Whalley. *At the end of the book is added all the Jacobinical publications which have issued from that shop of sedition; among these advertisements stands that of his famous controversy.*

The whole neighbourhood is up in arms, wrote Hannah, who was worried that the new prime minister, Henry Addington, would share the prejudices of his brother, Hiley Addington, at Langford Court.[62] In April she wrote to Whalley: *Patty has had a bullying sort of letter from Mr Parsons, for accusing his wife of falsehood: It is not yet answered, for one does not know how to deal with such vulgar, unprincipled people. It looks as if it came from some pettifogging attorney.* But, by the autumn, Mr Parsons had changed sides and Hannah was rallying other supporters in the village. *Farmer Young, Baber, etc,* she told Whalley, *should confine their affidavits to the defence of the Master and the School, and not attack Bere, lest he find out some stratagem to threaten a legal revenge. He will stick at nothing. If Mary Clarke could be got at, Sarah Dirrick, Filer, Huish, and, above all, Mrs Parker,* [and] *the bribing story which Descury knows, it must content us; but I fear we can't get it.*

The pamphlet war and the *Anti-Jacobin Review*

Sir Abraham soon agreed *to undertake the very unpleasant task of making some reply to this most base and artful book,* which he first sent Dr Whalley for his approval. *A Letter to the Rev. Thomas Bere, Rector of Butcombe, Occasioned by his Late Unwarrantable Attack on Mrs Hannah More ... By the Rev. Sir Abraham Elton Bart* was printed in June and sold at bookshops in London and Bath. Although Sir Abraham Elton's pamphlet was couched in rhetoric, Hannah retained her high opinion of him. Patty, however, felt that Sir Abraham was a liability and she was not the only one to find fault with him. *Sir Abraham evidently exults in his fancied superiority over his adversary in fluency of language and harmony of stile,* said the reviewer of his pamphlet in the *Anti-Jacobin Review, and his account displays a degree of triumph which had better been concealed. ... His adulation of*

Mrs More is gross, fulsome and offensive ... Sir Abraham may, if he pleases, fall prostrate before the shrine of the idol which he has raised up to himself: and lavish his incense with senseless profusion. The *Anti-Jacobin Review* had also discovered that Sir Abraham had been *refused ordination, on his first application to the Bishop* because of his *known attachment to the tenets and practices of Methodism, and that he actually preached in a Tabernacle before he was admitted to the pale of the Church.*[63] He and Eliza had, a year after their marriage, joined a Nonconformist Tabernacle in Penn Street, Bristol, founded by George Whitefield.[64]

From 1800 to 1803 a total of 23 pamphlets were published both for and against Hannah More.[65] Bere answered Elton's with a second, more abusive pamphlet; Elton answered that; others joined the fray; and the *Anti-Jacobin* reviewers became increasingly offensive. The *British Critic*, despite its High Church sympathies, supported Hannah and opposed the *Anti-Jacobin,* and opponents in the *Blagdon Controversy* could not safely be invited to meet at the same table.[66] But the dispute was no longer about a village Sunday school teacher for it now concerned the reputation of Hannah More and the future of all her schools and the Evangelical movement within the Church of England.

Wilberforce's *Practical View,* published in 1797, had become the classic text on the theology of Anglican Evangelicals. In 1798 the High Church clergyman Charles Daubeny had published his *Guide to the Church,* which was critical of this theology and attacked Dissenters and Calvinists. In 1799 Daubeny criticised More's *Strictures*[67] in his pamphlet, *A Letter to Mrs Hannah More,* in which he said, *Madam, this is not the language either of Scripture or of the Church of England*[68] This pamphlet was reviewed in the next issue of the *Anti-Jacobin Review* by his friend the High Church clergyman Jonathan Boucher, who quoted Daubeny almost word for word: *If Mrs More be really of Mr Wilberforce's school, her faith is, like his, Calvinism in disguise; and her attachment to the Church of England of a very doubtful kind.*[69]

This was not to be the last time that Hannah was chastised by Jonathan Boucher, aided and abetted by his friend, Charles Daubeny. In April 1800 Daubeny had told Boucher how *Mrs H: M: keeps a sort of school for the younger clergy ... This hop, skip & jump Divinity, as I call it, never fails to be accompanied with much confidence, self importance, and consequent contempt of all who do not study in the same school with themselves.*[70] In August 1801 an *Anti-Jacobin* reviewer, probably Boucher, revealed the existence of an *organized federation* [to increase] *the number of Methodists; by training them in the Church; of purchasing small livings for them* [so that they could pervert the doctrines of the Gospel as taught by the Church of England]; *we have long had indisputable proofs. Clapham Common*[71] *is their seat of power.*[72]

Bere's friend William Shaw, the Rector of Chelvey, spoke in his first pamphlet of *some agency yet invisible to the public* [the Bishop of London] though visible, said the *Anti-Jacobin Review, to ourselves and some others.* The reviewer, probably Boucher, continued to *blame severely all the parties hostile to Mr Bere:* Dr Crossman, *the reptile has crept deeper into the mud, and buried himself completely in it;* Bishop Moss was *contradictory, violent and cruel;* and the chancellor acted as if prompted by another bishop. *Every parish may be convulsed, and every Clergy-man may be oppressed, if the cunning of Mrs More can thus ... conjure up even good spirits, even the very angels of the church, to do her work of mischief for her ... in all the glory of a good angel ... able to "Ride in the whirlwind and direct the storm".*[73]

In September 1801 an anonymous pamphlet was published: *A statement of facts relative to Mrs H More's schools occasioned by some late misrepresentations* is now believed to have been written by John Boak. It contained the statements of nine clergy from five parishes where Hannah had schools and who were known to her enemies as "Hannah More's ninepins". The idea probably came from a High Churchman, Francis Randolph, who was the principal resident of Banwell and the proprietor of Laura Chapel, which the sisters attended in Bath. He had preached at Shipham Club feast in July when he had the opportunity to speak to the nine clergymen. His wife was an equally energetic ally and successfully sold More's version of the *Blagdon Controversy* to the royal family.[74]

Final closure of Blagdon Sunday school and the pamphlet war continued[75]

Meanwhile Mr Bere refused to vacate his curacy and was reinstated. Hannah wrote to Whalley: *Poor Patty goes to-morrow once more formally to dissolve the unfortunate Blagdon school. I have gone on so long to show that it was not abolished in resentment, and I go on no longer, in conformity with my principle of not acting against the resident clergyman ... Though my health is much impaired, I keep myself quiet, by neither reading any of the compositions of the adversaries, nor even allowing myself to talk on the subject.*

In October Mrs Piozzi wrote to Whalley: *Keep up our valuable friend Hannah's spirits ... The world is sick of such a long controversy ... It may now be handsomely dropped, and lost among the heaps of sense and nonsense, spite and panegyric, which this newer and more interesting subject, Peace,*[76] *will bury in oblivion.* However another year passed before the *controversy* was *handsomely dropped.*

In January 1802 the Bath layman, Edward Spencer, published his *Truths respecting Mrs Hannah More's Meeting-houses, and the Conduct of her Followers,* which even the *Anti-Jacobin* considered the most offensive yet. Spencer referred to Hannah the *She-Bishop,* who had changed Robert Raikes' admirable concept of Sunday schools into the most powerful engine of sectarianism; who supported Methodism and had taken communion at Jay's dissenting chapel in Bath; and whose *anniversary meetings of fanatic sectaries on the peak of a mountain* [on Mendip] would lead to Jacobin assemblies. The lawyers agreed that it was *actionable, and extremely wicked in a moral view*, but Hannah was against prosecution which was uncertain and would add to her distress.

In February Dr Whalley, who was then in London recovering after the death of his wife, kept himself busy by writing his own pamphlet. Patty wrote to him from Bath: *We admire the rapidity of your genius in getting everything so forward in such a little time ... We are now truly glad we agreed together, that you should entirely omit all mention of Lady Huntingdon,*[77] *etc; and we also wish you would neither notice Laura Chapel, nor Jay's, upon any consideration, as it would be running our heads into hornets' nests.* Hannah did not want Whalley to go into detail, only to say that it was *the general tendency and design of* [their] *schools to counteract Methodism, by bringing the common people to church*, as they had become lazy in recent years, and Patty suggested that he should ask, *Where are now the 150 or 200 children of Blagdon that used to occupy such a large space of your church?* They wanted him to confine himself to exposing Bere's actions and his motives; *the less praise given to* [Hannah] *and the less general invective the better;* Patty, who thought that Sir Abraham had hurt their cause by being too general and verbose suggested that the more he compressed, the better, and Hannah was anxious that the pamphlet should not *betray her knowledge of it.*

Hannah was again unwell and Patty told Whalley: *Dr Lovell ... shook his head at my poor sister; though the ague is much diminished, yet the bowels are very alarming.* Soon Patty was ill too and Sally More took over the letters to Whalley: *Frequently we thought* [Patty] *was gone for ever; she complained of a sudden pain in her thumb; in an instant she fell, from fainting fits etc.* Patty's illness made Hannah worse and *her complaints made such a general attack upon her* [that the sisters were] *thrown into the utmost terror ... She mentioned a certain pamphlet which is eagerly expected,* wrote Sally, *but I strongly suspect she thinks she shall never live to hear the reading of it; but I will not despair, so often as she has been raised from such desperate maladies.*

By March 1802, after a year of the *Blagdon Controversy*, the public were losing interest and Mrs Leeves wrote, in a *friendly letter* to the sisters, that Mr Bere's *partisans in the country* [were] *falling off daily: four or five new pamphlets are now in the press, some for, some against; one, I hear is by a clergyman of fortune, who intends to prove the deep scheme is all Atheism against Christianity; one of the pamphlets is entitled, amongst other names, "A Squint at St Hannah."*

Whalley's animadversions and the Rev. Sir Archibald MacSarcasm's *Life of Hannah More*

Meanwhile, in Bath, Sally More found her sister Mary *in great agitation cutting open a pamphlet just arrived from Hazard's* [bookshop] *entitled "Animadversions," etc. I have been running up and down ever since, catching a page of it as I can, from a lady who is reading it to Patty in her bed, all equally wondering who can be the author.* But Sally was teasing Whalley, as they knew it was the anonymous pamphlet which he had been writing in London: *Animadversions on the Curate of Blagdon's Three Publications ... with Some Allusions to his Cambrian Descent.* Soon the invalids were much better and Sally wrote that the pamphlet exceeded expectations: *Such a multitude of facts which can never be controverted. I have yet seen only a few friends, who are all animated on the subject ... I was in Hazard's shop when the Dean of Wells came in to make a purchase of the book ... Little Dr Shepherd - half mad, half Methodist, whom you must know - I saw him throw down the pamphlet, and heard him exclaim: "Complete detection - complete detection. Now it is all out";* then turning to me, he repeated the same. You may be assured of our inviolable secrecy, but I cannot answer that suspicion will never glance towards you.* Sally wrote again to Whalley to enquire whether Hatchard's bookshop in Piccadilly had sent his pamphlet to the Reviews, *particularly the Anti-Jacobin* [which planned] *to review the whole this month? ... All our friends* [in Bath] *are in high approbation of the work, and I find it is doing considerable mischief among the enemy; some inveterate spirits have been converted to the right faith* [Evangelical] *... not the slightest suspicion towards the author ... With the united compliments of the sisterhood.* Hannah, who had just read the pamphlet, wrote from her bed: *Nothing has escaped you* [and] *the writing is admirable. Sir A E suspects you ... God bless you, my dear sir. Nobody can feel more sensibly than I do how much I owe you ... The "Animadversions" were not got to Bristol when we heard ... I hope Hatchard will send it thither, and to Wells etc.*[78]

The review of *Animadversions* in the *Anti-Jacobin*, however, considered it to be *replete with the most low, vulgar, and scurrilous abuse of Mr Bere and his friends, and with the most fulsome adulation of Mrs More ... If all the stores of Grub-street had been rifled, they could not have produced ... matter more disgusting, more disgraceful, or more stupid.*[79] Not to mention the *low, vulgar, and scurrilous abuse* that was used against Hannah by Edward Spencer and the viciousness of Bere's friend William Shaw, who published a second pamphlet in 1802.

William Shaw, the Rector of Chelvey, together with Thomas Bere, *had emissaries in all the villages, who were sent to pick up any stories they could against me; his object being to destroy my remaining schools,* Hannah wrote to Wilberforce, *I had hoped to mollify him by silence; far from it; he has ventured ten times greater lengths from the certainty of not being contradicted.*[80] Shaw and Bere were obviously muck-raking for Shaw's viciously comic *Life of Hannah More, with a Critical Review of her Writings, by the Rev. Sir Archibald*

MacSarcasm Bart, who purported to be the brother of Sir Abraham Elton. It was the most humiliating attack on Hannah and Sir Abraham in the entire *Controversy*. The two clergymen "discovered" that Hannah had three former lovers: a strolling player, a sea captain and a soldier. *Sir Archibald* described his "brother" as Mrs More's faithful ally in persecution and cruelty and, as to his strange speech at the George Inn, *the more we read it the less we know of its subject*. His references to the ancient lineage of the house of MacSarcasms were unkind, as the Eltons had only recently risen to the ranks of the gentry,[81] as were those about Hannah More's parents, but these were no more unkind than Whalley's *Allusions to* [Mr Bere's] *Cambrian Descent* in his *Animadversions*. The *Anti-Jacobin* commented in August that Bere and Mrs More *may both congratulate themselves on having, by their own personal exertions and merits, raised themselves* [from humble beginnings] *to a higher station in life*.[82] This pamphlet showed the *Anti-Jacobin* that not all High Church clergy were Tory loyalists and the reviewer was convinced that Mr Bere would read it with indignation.

The retreat of the Anti-Jacobin Review

The *Anti-Jacobin* had announced in February 1802 that it would expose *the secret manoeuvres of the false friends to the church* [that is the bishops, particularly Porteus].[83] However, in the April issue, it was apparent that the *secret and powerful influence* had been brought to bear on the *Anti-Jacobin* and, whereas the review continued to attack Crossman, Moss and Mrs More, it gave up its attack on the Bishop of London, who was opposed to Calvinism and had become increasingly anxious about his association with Hannah. Porteus was enigmatically referred to as one for whom the review had a *peculiar veneration* but who appeared *to have been induced … from his general correctness of opinion … by his esteem for a writer* [Mrs More] *whose cunning … could not always have concealed from **his** eye the Calvinism which it has betrayed to ours*.[84] In March 1800 Boucher had accused Hannah More of *listening to unauthorised preachers and frequenting other places of worship than the established church*[85] and in April 1802 came the damaging revelation: *the positive fact of* [Hannah's] *having received THE SACRAMENT from the hands of a **Layman**.*[86] *It is fearful to think of,* wrote William Cobbett, *that this woman had under her tuition the children of a large portion of England.*[87]

Patty was finding it difficult *to keep everything from* [Hannah] *and at the same time not to appear ungrateful to her ardent friends.*[88] However, in April Bishop Moss died and was replaced by Dr Beadon, Bishop of Gloucester, who had subscribed to Hannah's *Cheap Repository Tracts.* Before he had even arrived in Wells, she took the opportunity to present her case to him in a very long letter[89] to which he replied, offering her remaining schools his protection and encouragement, so long as they were *under the inspection and guidance of* [herself] *and the several parochial ministers.*[90] With Dr Beadon and other High Church bishops, as well as most of the Mendip clergy, supporting her, More's enemies were forced to retreat.

In September 1802 the *Anti-Jacobin Review* at last realised their mistake: Hannah More was not a subversive enemy of the Church and State but an ultra loyalist, and that, despite her Evangelicalism, she had the support of eminent High Churchmen. In 1803 Daubeny, who had suggested to Boucher the infamous phrase "*Calvinism in disguise*", quickly disassociated himself from Boucher and the reviewers and credited the phrase to them.[91] *It is from no kindness to* **me** *that the anti-Jacobin has changed its note,* Hannah wrote to Wilberforce, *but they are frightened for themselves, now that the world has found out what are the real principles, religious and political of the party they have so zealously espoused ... Peace be with them. Their repentance comes too late to do me any good.* But the reviews and letters, for and against Hannah More, continued until December 1803 when an observant eye-witness wrote an account of the Shipham Club feast, attended by at least *two hundred poor women, respectable and neatly dressed ... and a great number of poor children ... Well, I said, here is no methodism; here is no faith without works; here is not ... any Calvinism ... I felt strongly ... such temporal benefits bestowed (as nearly every child had some clothing on provided by the charity), such kindness and exertion conferred, merited not the obloquy Miss H M had received.*[92]

Hannah More in 1809 © The National Portrait Gallery, London

So the *Blagdon Controversy* ended: Blagdon had lost its Sunday school, but Hannah More still had eight other schools, and Thomas Bere was still the Curate of Blagdon. Today it appears to be little more than a storm in a tea cup, but in the context of its time it had a very different appearance and rang alarm bells in many people's ears. In 1798 the Wedmore farmers had highlighted two issues: *Methody* and *rebellion* - the same issues to be raised by the *Anti-Jacobin Review*. At a local level the Controversy was about religion: whether her teachers were Methodists and whether Hannah More was a Methodist.

The Established Church's fear of Methodism and itinerant preachers

John Wesley (1703-1791) had arrived in Bristol in 1739 to continue the work begun by George Whitefield (1714-1770). Both were Church of England clergymen who had been influenced by the Moravians, a small protestant sect. Wesley's preaching soon attracted dissenters and Anglicans to join religious societies in private homes which he organised on Moravian lines. As membership increased, he bought a patch of land and built what he called their new room in the Horsefair. The room, which was used as a schoolroom and dispensary for poor people as well as for worship, meetings and conferences, was the first Methodist chapel and is still known as the New Room. Although Wesley reached across denominational boundaries, he wanted to keep "Methodism" within the Anglican Church, rather than compete with it, so Methodist meetings were always outside church hours and the Methodists did not separate from the Church until after Wesley's death in 1791.

Whitefield began open-air preaching in the Bristol area in 1739 but Wesley, who had *thought the saving of souls almost a sin if it had not been done in church,*[93] was reluctant to follow his example. But he soon realised that he could save more souls if he preached outdoors and reached people, such as the large number of colliers at Kingswood, where there were few parish churches. His first outdoor service attracted some 3,000 people to St Philip's Marsh.

Wesley's open-air ministry became very concerned with the spiritual welfare of the poor, who felt oppressed by the Corn Laws, turnpike taxes, low wages and, especially in the 1790s, by high bread prices due to poor harvests. The Kingswood colliers were rough, unruly workers who had taken part in turnpike and grain riots, but Wesley considered them neglected people. His other supporters were mostly artisans and tradespeople, especially shoemakers (like Henry Young), servants and shopkeepers, and many were women. Many poor people were disillusioned with the Anglican Church or felt excluded from it. The Church also lacked the excitement, congregational involvement and emotional spirit of the dissenting Churches, which offered them a chance to seek a better life and taught that salvation could be earned by good conduct and morals. Membership of these churches did not depend on birth but commitment and piety and the Sunday schools attached to dissenting chapels offered the poor a chance to learn to read and write.

Wesley delivered his sermons in language which working people could understand, with practical relevance and ethical advice, and he seemed to have a message for every individual. The poor people in Blagdon thought *that Mr Young could explain the scriptures better than Mr Bere, a thousand times better,* and one of his *private scholars,* John Baker, *had been for a week to Bristol to hear the methodists and liked them desperate ... he never heard such preaching in his life.*[94] However, emotional scenes which were common in the early years gave Methodism a bad name. Tears, convulsions and visions of God often occurred when John Wesley preached and paroxysms and groanings occasionally occurred when Whitefield or Charles Wesley preached. The Anglican Church and the Bristol Corporation, alarmed by this spirit of "enthusiasm", saw Methodism as a threat to religious order and perhaps feared a return to the religious fanaticism of the 17th century. Attacks on Methodism appeared in pamphlets and in Bristol papers, which were sometimes read by Mendip farmers. But, despite opposition, Methodism survived in Bristol and spread into the countryside, particularly the Mendips, due to Wesley's circuit system, which assigned itinerant preachers, mostly laymen, to seven circuits. These preachers travelled round the country preaching in the open air or at private meetings and, as their numbers grew, so did the area they could cover. They didn't need qualifications, only evidence of their conversion to Christ, a passion for the salvation of their congregation and an ability to communicate their faith in simple terms.

Henry Young had all the qualities of a Methodist preacher and his Monday evening school resembled the class discipline of the Methodists. But it was hard to find good male teachers, especially "spiritual teachers," and, although Hannah was wary of appointing teachers who showed signs of the "enthusiasm" associated with Methodism, she preferred this to formal religion. Wilberforce had advised her to use Methodists when she could not find Evangelicals and she later admitted to him that Young *was a disciple of John Wesley's.*[95] Sarah Baber, the Methodist teacher at Cheddar, had been appointed before the Methodists separated from the Church but Henry Young and John Harvard, the Wedmore teacher, were appointed after the split.[22] Harvard was so indiscreet that Hannah dismissed him and transferred Mrs Caroll from Axbridge to Wedmore, where she too was accused of Methodism.[96]

The Church of England tolerated Methodism when it brought religion to neglected parishes but not when it led people away from the Church, so church attendance was part of the discipline of all Hannah More's schools. Methodists on the Mendips worried that these schools were rivals to their own meetings, so it was Hannah's *avowed object to counteract the Methodists* as her enemies.[97] She told Whalley that *the Wrington Methodists* [were] *ever on the watch to see where they* [could] *slip in,* [and] *attempt to draw away some of our poor people from church, to which ... Young* [had] *hitherto kept them firm.*[98]

But was Young a Calvinist? Hannah wrote to Wilberforce, *It makes me almost sick to tell you that the Blagdon Inquisition have driven our poor schoolmaster to take an oath that he is not a Calvinist! It is a nickname. They do not at all know what it means.*[99] Whitefield was a Calvinist and he believed in absolute predestination – only certain elect Christians would be saved, however wicked they might be. Wesley was an Armenian Methodist who believed in conditional predestination – anyone could be saved, if they had faith. After 1742 the Calvinists and the Armenians held separate services, but by the 1790s the term "Calvinist" was used indiscriminately, as in Blagdon, to refer to anyone who was a Methodist, a fanatic or an "enthusiast". Although Hannah mistrusted *enthusiasm*, she excused it in the poor, as *the coarse way* in which illiterates, who have become religious, express themselves. Their enthusiasm was *only vulgarity or quaintness* and *not a reason why the poor should be left destitute of religious instruction* and given up to *vice and barbarism.*[89] In 1799 the *Anti-Jacobin Review* implied that the term *Calvinist* had the same meaning as it had during the English Civil War, which had led to the execution of Charles I.

The More sisters were not Methodists and there is no evidence that they ever met the Wesleys. They were brought up as Anglicans and later joined the Evangelical group within the Anglican Church, which originated with the Vicar of Clapham. But they tolerated Nonconformity, believing the Church of Christ included all denominations, and they attended the dissenting chapel of William Jay in Bath, even taking communion there. Patty explained to Dr Whalley: *Before we came from Bristol we had never thought of going anywhere but to church,* [but when they came to Bath in 1790, the churches were badly filled.] *Jay was then in all his glory, and little else talked of; his chapel was full, and half filled by people from church, I mean on a Sunday evening. I have seen great numbers of clergymen there, and often Dr Randolf* [sic]. *All this was thought nothing of by anybody; Jay's orthodoxy and talents bore everything before it, nor was the thing remarked, that ever I heard of, till the French Revolution, when Tom Paine, etc, began to show their cloven feet ... At this time the cry of the Church began to come forward, and all those harmless admirers of Jay withdrew as the prejudices of the people began to break out. ... what may surprise you more,* wrote Patty, *I know many High Church people ... who have always the Church prayers performed morning and evening in their family, did the same* [as the More sisters] *without ... its ever occurring to them they had done any wrong thing.*[100]

The French Revolution, when "Tom Paine, etc, began to show their cloven feet"

The *Blagdon Controversy* unfortunately coincided with the French Revolution and loyalist panic in England. The Wedmore farmer's fear, that the day *the school was opened would be the beginning of such rebellion in England as had taken place in Ireland and France,* was an exaggeration, but "Britons in the 1790s were facing a highly volatile situation that looked very dangerous indeed to those persons living through it."[101]

The storming of the Bastille in Paris, which marked the beginning of the French Revolution in 1789, took place only a month before Wilberforce decided that *something must be done for Cheddar.*[102] In October, while Hannah and Patty were busy setting up their first Mendip Sunday school, a starving mob of Paris market women marched on Versailles and reached the Queen's apartments, protesting about the shortage and the high price of bread. Louis XVI, Queen Marie Antoinette and their children became hostages of the Revolution at the Tuileries in Paris.

French aristocrats who had fled the Revolution terrified the English landed classes. Many landowners, who had recently enclosed their estates and driven the poor off the commons, feared new ideas about human rights. Edmund Burke, a friend of the More family since their Park Street days, had risen into the landed gentry and represented their interests in parliament. In 1790 he published his *Reflections on the Revolution in France*, a passionate attack on the revolutionaries, which warned Britons against the dangers of mob rule and the breakdown of civilisation. It sold nearly 20,000 copies in six months.

Others in England had great hopes of the Revolution. Among them was Mary Wollstonecraft whose *Vindication of the Rights of Man* criticised Burke's *flowers of rhetoric* as the most dangerous enemy of human rights. Her pamphlet sold for half the price of Burke's and was soon followed by her *Vindication of the Rights of Woman. Women awake!* she rallied. *The tocsin of enlightenment and reason resounds through the universe; recognise your rights.* This provoked outrage in England and Hannah More, despite her views on female education, was not impressed: *I have been pestered to read 'The Rights of Women', but am invincibly resolved not to do it,* she assured Horace Walpole. *There is something fantastic and absurd in the very title.*[103]

Tom Paine's *Rights of Man,* which called for the abolition of monarchy and aristocracy and advocated an egalitarian republic, sold 200,000 copies by 1793, causing alarm amongst loyalists. British radicals joined reforming societies, which copied the more dangerous French societies: the Society for Constitutional Information was revived in 1791; and the artisan-based London Corresponding

Society, for the encouragement of constitutional discussion, which was formed in 1792 by a master cobbler, distributed *The Rights of Man* to the working classes. The Constitutional Society spread its ideas through radical pamphlets, while the Corresponding Society, like the French Jacobin Club,[104] had daughter associations in other towns, but their aim was electoral reform not revolution or regicide. They called for manhood suffrage, annual parliaments, cheaper government, a cheaper legal system and the end of unjust land enclosures.

In April 1792, while Hannah and Patty set up their school in Nailsea, France declared war on Austria and Prussia. In May the British government, alarmed by reports of unrest amongst the working classes in Paris, encouraged magistrates to be rigorous in controlling riotous meetings and seditious publications. In August Patty wrote in her journal, *We now began to occupy our thoughts in planning clubs for poor women,*[105] while in Paris an insurrection of shop-keepers, tradesmen and artisans, with the National Guard, stormed the Tuileries and slaughtered the King's Swiss Guard. Many ordinary people were killed or wounded; the royal family was taken prisoner; for two days the shops were shut, people were confined to their homes and 3,000 people were arrested. In September Patty described their day of procession at Cheddar where *Mr Boak gave us a most suitable sermon, and we returned from church as we went, preceded by one hundred and fifty-eight children, who were also solaced with a good plum-tart.*[106] Meanwhile, in Paris, over 1,000 priests and political prisoners were murdered, universal suffrage was recognised and tensions mounted between moderates and radicals. In December Louis XVI, accused of conspiring with counter-revolutionaries against France, was tried by the Convention. Many English residents in Paris, including William Wordsworth, now left in panic.

In Britain William Pitt, alarmed by mass meetings of radicals and the growing probability of war with France, mobilised the militia and called parliament into special session. Prosecutions of writers, printers and sellers of seditious literature led to the conviction of Tom Paine, who fled to France but was tried in his absence and found guilty: his effigies were burned in different parts of England including Axbridge. The counter-revolutionary Crown and Anchor Association was founded with government aid and local branches sprang up in the country to help the government eradicate sedition.

At the beginning of 1793, Patty wrote in her journal: *Our great joy and pleasure ... is the apparent turning from a life of wickedness to a life of righteousness ... in the case of Mr Hyde ... our great persecutor.*[107] In France Louis XVI was found guilty and was beheaded by the new guillotine before a crowd of 80,000. In February France declared war on Great Britain and most of the remaining English in Paris rushed home in a second wave of panic.

While the More sisters entertained Wilberforce and the Rector of Clapham at Cowslip Green, the dictatorship under Robespierre marked the end of democracy in France. The few Britons who remained in Paris were now considered enemy aliens and even Mary Wollstonecraft became disillusioned. Robespierre was brought to power by the most radical group in France, the Jacobin Club, which - although initially moderate - embraced the cause of the working classes. *Terror* now became the "order of the day" in France: 250 Britons, including Tom Paine, were imprisoned in Paris as spies or counter-revolutionaries; huge numbers went to the guillotine every day including, in October, Queen Marie Antoinette. In Somerset Dr and Mrs Whalley must have recalled their visit to Versailles in 1783 with great sadness. The French queen had then been particularly struck by the handsome Dr Whalley, whom she named *le bel Anglais*.[108]

In April 1794 all foreigners had to leave Paris within ten days or be executed, and by the time Robespierre was overthrown, some 300,000 suspects had been arrested, about 17,000 had been executed and the Place de Revolution had become a blood bath. In July Robespierre fell from power and was executed with many other Jacobins.

Dr Thomas Sedgwick Whalley - le bel Anglais

The Terror ended, but France was still at war with the monarchies of Europe and foreigners were still the enemy. Soon the Jacobin Club was closed, the salons and theatres reopened and Mary Wollstonecraft returned to Paris to find all the English had gone.

Shock-waves from across the Channel cause panic in England

Horrific reports of the Revolution appeared in English newspapers and news also reached England through refugee French nobility and clergy. One emigre cleric, Abbé Barruel, published a history of Jacobinism in 1794, which claimed that the French Revolution was the culmination of a grand international plot led by Freemasons, philosophers and Bavarian illuminati. A similar book, *Proofs of a Conspiracy against all the Religions and Governments of Europe* by a Scottish professor and future Anti-Jacobin reviewer, was believed by many English bishops.

Panic spread through divergent groups in the British government, which united under the Tory leader, William Pitt, in fear of radicalism and treason at home. In May 1794 twelve leading members of the Society for Constitutional Information and the London Corresponding Society were arrested for high treason, which was punishable by death. In October Pitt instigated Treason Trials for the twelve accused, but they were all acquitted to the jubilation of the reform clubs, who held a mass meeting in London, causing so much alarm that the cavalry were held at the ready.

In March 1795 the remains of the British army were driven back to England by the French, who reached the coast of the Low Countries and then camped at Boulogne to convince Pitt that they were preparing to invade England. The debilitating effects of the war and a series of cold winters and poor harvests caused scarcity and unrest in the country. The winter of 1794-5 was one of the worst in the century, with bitterly cold weather lasting into March, and the poor were in great distress. In October, not long after Hannah had opened her Blagdon Sunday school, George III's coach was stoned in London by crowds demonstrating against the war with France, crying, *Bread! Peace! No Pitt!*

The government, determined to recover authority, had already temporarily suspended the Habeas Corpus Act to allow political suspects to be held without trial. Parliament next passed two new acts: the Seditious Meetings Act restricted public meetings and the Treasonable Practices Act extended the definition of treason. The Home Office advised that a knowledge of local conditions was important for the effective administration of the latter and the government soon had secret agents everywhere, even in Somerset.

West Country radicals[109]

Early in 1795 the poet Samuel Taylor Coleridge, then aged 22, gave three political lectures in Bristol, which were critical of Pitt's government. These were followed in the summer by a series of lectures at the Assembly Coffee House on Bristol Quay, which compared the English Civil War and the French Revolution. The radical nature of these lectures made him friends amongst the prosperous nonconformist community, who sympathised with the social aims of the French Revolution, but also made him many enemies.

In December 1796 Coleridge moved, with his wife and baby, to a cottage in Nether Stowey. In the same month a French invasion fleet, in league with the United Irishmen,[110] sailed for Ireland and only bad weather and bad seamanship prevented their landing. Then, in January, the people of North Devon were alarmed when three French frigates and a lugger were sighted off Ilfracombe making their way up the Bristol Channel with the apparent intention of burning Bristol with its bridges, docks, warehouses and factories. However they were driven off by the North Devon Volunteers and only a contrary wind prevented them from attacking Bristol. In February 1797 they landed at Fishguard and surrendered two days later, but the West Country and the government remained anxious, especially as there were two mutinies in the Royal Navy's own fleet in April and May.

On 11th August 1797 the government's top agent, John Walsh, was sent to Somerset to investigate the suspicious activities of two poets near Bridgwater, whom they feared might be marking likely landing places for the French. Coleridge had abandoned politics in dismay but his radical reputation went with him to Stowey and the villagers were very suspicious of the *vile Jacobin villain* who took long walks in the hills with a pencil and notebook. His friend, William Wordsworth, had witnessed the jubilant early years of the French Revolution but had been disillusioned by the later atrocities and moved, with his sister Dorothy, to a house in Alfoxden, not far from Stowey.

The locals in Nether Stowey were already suspicious of Coleridge and the visitors to his cottage when, in July, Wordsworth decided to hold a house-warming party to which he invited John Thelwall, a known atheist, mob orator and Jacobin. Both Coleridge and Thelwall were now disillusioned radicals who had turned their backs on active politics. Fourteen people sat down to dinner and the Wordsworths employed a local man, Thomas Jones, as waiter. When Mr Thelwall got up after dinner, wearing the white hat of a radical, he *talked so loud and was in such a Passion that Jones was frightened. ... The wiseacres of the village had ... made Mr W the subject of their serious conversation* and concluded that a man so given to wandering the hills at late hours *like a partridge* and looking strangely at the moon, must either be a conjurer, a smuggler, or *a desperd French Jacobin* who was spying out ground for a French invasion. Wordsworth probably never knew how his walks with Dorothy and Coleridge had been misrepresented. The gossip reached Charles Mogg, a former servant at Alfoxden, who was now cook for Dr Lysons of Bath and, when Dr Lysons heard the story he wrote to the Duke of Portland, the home secretary, alerting him to the *very suspicious business* taking place at Alfoxden. On 15th August John Walsh reached the Globe Inn at Stowey where the conversation at the bar quickly turned to *those rascals from Alfoxden* and John Thelwall, who had left for Bristol two weeks earlier. *I ... asked if they meant the famous Thelwall,* John Walsh reported. *They said yes. That he had been down some time, and that there were a Nest of them at Alfoxden House.* Assured that they were not French, he quickly concluded that he was dealing with *a mischievous gang of disaffected Englishmen.* For the next three weeks Walsh tracked the poets on their daily excursions into the hills and down to the beach at Kilve and then departed, much to the amusement of Coleridge. But Thelwall, who was one of the men acquitted at the Treason Trials, knew all too well that they had been in real danger.

The Anti-Jacobin Review

At this time of loyalist panic a group of bright young politicians met in a house in Piccadilly in 1797 where they began to write a weekly, anti-French, satirical newspaper called the *Anti-Jacobin.* They included the ambitious George Canning, the future prime minister, who had just been appointed under-secretary for foreign affairs, and John Hookham Frere, an under secretary at the Home Office. The editor, William Gifford, was privy to inside government information and the paper was printed by James Wright, to whose bookshop the house in Piccadilly was connected by a secret passage.[111]

The word *Jacobin,* which came from the radical Jacobin Club in Paris, was a creation of Pittite propaganda and was used indiscriminately by this loyalist paper to describe anyone who sympathised with the French Revolution or campaigned for political reform. It became an ominous catchword for subversion in all its forms. The purpose of the paper was to discredit the opponents to Pitt's unpopular war with France, which was a heavy tax burden, and was only supported by the British people because they feared a French invasion. The writers aimed to make their Whig opponents appear ridiculous by exposing the *Lies, Misrepresentations and Mistakes* in the previous week's liberal newspapers and by ridiculing "Jacobin" poets and writers: Coleridge, Erasmus Darwin and William Godwin were all parodied under the name of Mr William Higgins, an author residing at St Mary Axe. Coleridge's true birthplace was Ottery St Mary, near the river Axe.[111]

In July 1798 the weekly paper was replaced by a monthly *Anti-Jacobin Review*, a literary review with a mission to defend orthodoxy - political, religious, moral and social - from forces at home and abroad which threatened to destroy it. To the *Anti-Jacobin Review* the French Revolution was the *most dangerous enemy which ever disturbed the peace of the world*.[112] The review held the same ideology as the newspaper but, unlike the newspaper, its aim was to fight the lies of the Jacobin press, which was supporting and defending the Regicides of France and the Traitors of Ireland.[110] The new editor, John Gifford,[113] had published an anti-Jacobin *History of France 1791-4* and apparently edited the Tory-funded *True Britain* newspaper. The staff on both papers were mostly Burkean conservatives, though some went further than Burke in their acceptance of a conspiracy theory of Jacobinism on both sides of the channel to effect a revolution in Britain and Ireland. The bright young Canningite Tories of the newspaper were replaced by men with literary and journalistic experience, mostly from the parsonages of rural England. Consequently, the *Review* was just as vindictive as the paper, but it was humourless, preoccupied with religious controversy and fanatical about the dangers posed by the Jacobin movement.[114] It also became obsessed with Calvinism, parallels were drawn with the English civil war of the 1640s and Puritan doctrines were traced back to their source - *the French refugee Calvin*. Hence Boucher's concern that the faith of both Wilberforce and More was *Calvinism in disguise*.

By 1798 the war had begun to have a disturbing effect on the economy and there was a renewal of agitation. The Newspaper Publication Act put publishers under the close supervision of magistrates. In 1799 the Corresponding Society and similar bodies were suppressed and in 1799-1800 Pitt's Combination Acts outlawed all combinations of workmen to harass their employers.

The *Review* saw plots and conspiracies everywhere and in 1800 the Sunday school movement came under suspicion: George Pretyman, Bishop of Lincoln, commissioned a survey of his large diocese, which revealed *a wandering tribe of fanatical teachers from the lowest and most illiterate classes of society*.[115] In the same year, the High Church Bishop of Rochester, Samuel Horsley, in his *Charge ... to the Clergy of his Diocese* linked Sunday schools, Methodists and itinerant preachers in a Jacobin conspiracy:[116] *Schools of Jacobinical politics abound in this country. In them the minds of many of the lowest orders are taught to despise religion and the laws of subordination*.[117] *Sunday schools must be under clerical inspection and control*. Not surprisingly the *Anti-Jacobin* took up the same subject in its October issue:

... If, it was once argued, religion were taught to common people ... their reasoning would serve only to perplex their minds, and lead them off from their proper pursuits or occupations, till at length it terminated in methodism or infidelity ... After the lapse of a few years, the debate was no longer supported by speculation only. It appeared that a vast number of those, who have been brought up at Sunday-School, were wandering from their proper callings, had become fanatical

teachers, had deemed themselves qualified to hold disputations upon religious topics, were turned sceptics and infidels, and anarchists and were spreading a malignant influence through the mass of the community … Those who have been taught to read, write and reason [are] *now grasping with eager curiosity, every pernicious treatise within their reach … We fear that the abuses of* [Sunday schools] *have extended much more widely than* [the Bishop of Lincoln] *seems to apprehend.*[118] The publication of Thomas Bere's *Controversy* in March 1801 played right into their hands.

Hannah later admitted that her greatest mistake was that she did not instantly dismiss Young. *I thought myself bound to protect an innocent man,* she wrote to Dr Beadon in 1802, *whom I still consider to have been falsely accused, but I was convinced that, as the event proved, the object in view was not merely to ruin* **him,** *but to strike at the principle of all my schools and to stigmatize them as seminaries of fanaticism, vice and sedition.*

Both versions of the *Anti-Jacobin* enjoyed government support and the relationship between John Gifford and the government was, without doubt, of mutual benefit. He received two successive police magistracies, an annual Treasury pension and subsidies from the secret service.[119] This may have reinforced his allegiance to Pitt but he was already sincerely, even fanatically, loyal to the civil and religious establishments and opposed to the French Revolution and the English reform movement. Some of the paper's other contributors enjoyed government patronage, such as Treasury subsidies, crown livings and civil service places, but they were all completely sincere in their opinions.[120] Both papers included prints by the caricaturist, James Gillray, illustrating the horrors of French Jacobinism and the imagined horrors of a French invasion. He also received a secret government pension. It is impossible to say for certain whether the *Anti-Jacobin* and William Cobbett's paper, *Porcupine* - which also criticised Hannah – were sponsored by right wing elements in Pitt's coalition, as Secret Service accounts used for press subsidisation after mid–1793 are lost.[121]

Once the *Blagdon Controversy* was taken up by the London journals, it acquired a political significance and the Mendip schools were caught in the crossfire between radicals and loyalists. *The loss of our idol, Pitt, was a blow that required firmer nerves than I possess to sustain with equanimity,* Hannah wrote to Whalley in February 1801, *I could be ready almost to apply to him Antony's superb encomium on Caesar – He was the foremost man of all this world.*[122] Was this the remark of a Jacobin radical? Or was it the voice of Hannah More, the supporter of Burke and author of *Village Politics*, and the Cheap Repository Tracts,[123] which taught the poor that they should be content with the station in life to which God had allotted them? As Dr Beadon put it to her: *I can only say, if you are not a sincere and zealous friend to the constitutional establishment both in Church and State, you are one of the greatest hypocrites, as well as one of the best writers, in his Majesty's dominions.*[124]

Hannah More's reputation survived the *Blagdon Controversy* because her network of friends, built up over many years, supported her. Despite her efforts to spread the Evangelical message and to promote "gospel" preachers, she retained the support of High Church bishops as well as the local clergy and her enemies retreated. Most of the remaining schools, purged of any taint of Methodism, survived and flourished and, while Blagdon had lost its Sunday school and its school of industry, Hannah claimed she had transformed Blagdon into a law-abiding, church-going community. Henry Young went to Ireland and was found a post by the Evangelical La Touche family[125] and Thomas Bere remained curate until his death in 1803, two months before the death of George Crossman and *on nearly the same day* as Thomas Drewitt, the Evangelical Curate of Cheddar. *B was called away to answer at the bar of God, for a life spent in opposition to the light of knowledge and education,* Hannah wrote in her diary on 3rd November. *Both called to eternity together! O how different the account they had to give of their respective talents.*[126]

In 1801 the More sisters had bought a plot of land at Barley Wood in Wrington where they built a house in the fashionable cottage style, with a thatched roof and a wide veranda round the first storey, similar to Mendip Lodge.

Barley Wood

They moved there in September 1801 and were so happy that they sold their house in Bath. Four of the sisters died at Barley Wood and, after Patty's death in 1819, Hannah stayed on alone until 1828. She left her beloved Barley Wood reluctantly, as she was having problems with *ungrateful and dishonest domestics,* and moved to a new house in Windsor Terrace, Clifton - then a new suburb of Bristol - which belonged to Thomas Sedgwick Whalley. Hannah More died there in 1833, at the age of 88, and was buried with her sisters in Wrington churchyard.

References

Abbreviations:

MM Martha More, *Mendip Annals, or, the Narrative of the Charitable Labours of Hannah and Martha More*, ed. Arthur Roberts, London 1859.

TB Thomas Bere, *The Controversy between Mrs Hannah More and the Curate of Blagdon, relative to the Conduct of her Teacher of the Sunday School in that Parish*, London 1801.

TW *The Journals and Correspondence of Thomas Sedgewick* [Sedgwick] *Whalley DD*, ed. Hill Wickham, 2 vols, London 1863.

Duke Duke University, North Carolina, Rare Book, Manuscript and Special Collections Library, William Wilberforce Papers.

AS Anne Stott, *Hannah More: The First Victorian*, Oxford University Press 2003.

AJR The *Anti-Jacobin Review*.

[1] Mrs was used as a term of respect for a mature woman. Hannah More never married.

[2] MM, pp.204-221.

[3] Evangelicals within the Established Church. (See Part 1 of this essay in *A History of Blagdon*, vol.2.)

[4] Patty was the nickname of Martha More, Hannah's younger sister, who helped her to set up the Mendip schools. Their three elder sisters were Mary, Elizabeth and Sarah (Sally).

[5] Enthusiasm was an 18th century term for fanaticism or extravagant religious emotion.

[6] It was alleged that Mr Bere was a Socinian — a follower of an early Protestant movement which rejected orthodox teachings on the Trinity and the divinity of Jesus and which held rationalistic views on sin and salvation.

[7] TB, pp.10-14.

[8] Bere to More, 3rd Dec 1796, Duke, cited in AS, p.165.

[9] An extempore prayer was an improvised prayer.

[10] MM, p.222.

[11] 4,809 parishes in England and Wales had non-resident clergy in 1815 and more than half of these had no parsonage. Parliamentary return for 1815 cited in Henry Thompson, *The Life of Hannah More with Notices of her Sisters*, London 1838, p.110.

[12] Bere to Crossman, 19th Jan 1801, TB, p.101.

[13] TB, pp.15-19.

[14] Patty More always wrote Henry Young's name as Younge.

[15] MM, pp.227-228.

[16] Margaret Elton, *Annals of the Elton Family: Bristol Merchants and Somerset Landowners*, Alan Sutton Publishing Ltd 1994, pp.108-111.

[17] The local magistrates met once a month at the Langford Inn.

[18] MM, pp.228-229.

[19] Margaret Elton, *Annals of the Elton Family: Bristol Merchants and Somerset Landowners*, Alan Sutton Publishing Ltd 1994, pp.113-114.

[20] TB, pp.20-40.

[21] A conventicle was a secret, illegal religious meeting.

[22] The Methodists had separated from the Anglican Church after Wesley's death in 1791 and the Church feared that they would take people away from its congregations.

[23] More to Dr Beadon, spring 1802, cited in William Roberts, *Memoirs of the Life and Correspondence of Hannah More*, 3rd ed., 1834, vol.3, pp.123-139.

[24] TB, pp.40-57.

[25] MM, p.55.

[26] More to Wilberforce, 29th Sep 1800, Duke, cited in AS, p.236.

[27] Clark, Hannah More MSS box 12, Bere to G P Seymour, 3rd Nov 1800, cited in AS, p.237.

[28] MM, p.239.

[29] More to Wilberforce, 28th Oct 1800, Duke, cited in AS, p.236.

[30] Patty More to Wilberforce, Duke, cited in AS, p.236.

[31] TB, pp.57-78.

[32] TW, pp.25.

[33] This was the time of the French Revolution and during the 1790s France had been at war with Austria, Prussia, the Netherlands, Britain and Spain.

[34] TB, pp.79-90.

[35] TW, p.200.

[36] TW, pp.25-26.

[37] TB, pp.82-84.

[38] TW, pp.145-146.

[39] TW, p.152.

[40] TW, pp.1-15.

[41] TW, pp.146-148, p.199.

[42] More to Wilberforce, 2nd Dec 1800, cited in William Roberts, *Memoirs of the Life and Correspondence of Hannah More*, 3rd ed., 1834, vol.3, p.145.

[43] More to Pretyman, 24th Sep 1800, Centre for Kentish Studies, Stanhope, cited in AS, p.247.

[44] TW, pp.147-151.

[45] AS, p.250.

[46] TB, pp.85-90.

[47] The church then had "a substantial tower ... a clock and 5 bells." John Collinson, *The History and Antiquities of the County of Somerset*, vol.3, p.570.

[48] TW, pp.154-166.

49 Mr Parsons' name first appears in the Vestry minutes in March 1785 when he attended the Easter meeting of principal inhabitants to elect the parish officers for the following year. The Vestry minutes for 1786-1807 are missing, but it is possible that Mr Parsons was Bere's churchwarden for some of this period.

50 TB, pp.91-99.

51 MM, p.19, p.29, p.44, p.206.

52 Anne Stott, *Hannah More: Evangelicalism, Cultural Reformation and Loyalism,* unpublished PhD Thesis, University College London, 1998, p.335.

53 Edward Spencer, *Truths respecting Mrs Hannah More's Meeting-houses, and the Conduct of her Followers,* January 1802.

54 TW, pp.164-171.

55 TW, pp.174-192.

56 Patty More to Sir Charles Middleton, 9th Feb 1801, cited in AS, p.238.

57 TB, pp.107-117.

58 TW, pp.181-2.

59 TW, p.162.

58 TB, pp.93-125.

59 TW, p.186.

60 TW, p.181.

61 TW, pp.188-194.

62 More to Wilberforce, 18th Mar 1801, Duke, cited in AS, p.238.

63 AJR, Jun 1801, vol.9, pp.289-95.

64 Margaret Elton, *Annals of the Elton Family: Bristol Merchants and Somerset Landowners,* Alan Sutton Publishing Ltd 1994, p.72.

65 MG Jones, *Hannah More,* Cambridge University Press, 1952, p.172.

66 Henry Thompson, *The Life of Hannah More with Notices of her Sisters,* London 1838.

67 Hannah More's *Strictures on the Modern System of Female Education,* published in 1799, aimed to improve the education of upper-class women, but also contained an avowal of her Evangelical theology.

68 Charles Daubeny, *A Letter to Mrs Hannah More on Some Part of her Late Publication Entitled "Strictures on Female Education",* Bath and London 1799, p.39.

69 AJR, Nov 1799, vol.4 pp.255-256.

70 Daubeny to Boucher,16 Apr 1800, MS Boucher, B/5/15, cited Anne Stott, *Hannah More: Evangelicalism, Cultural Reformation and Loyalism,* unpublished PhD Thesis, University College London, 1998, p.336.

71 The Evangelical movement within the Church of England was led by John Venn, the Vicar of Clapham, and later became known as the Clapham Sect.

72 AJR, Aug 1801, vol.10, p.390.

73 AJR, Aug 1801, vol.10, p.394.

74 AS, p.248.

75   TW, pp.201–215.

76   In March 1801 Pitt was succeeded by Henry Addington and, in the midst of food shortages and financial crisis and without allies, England was desperate for peace. Peace preliminaries were concluded on 1st October 1801 and the war ended with the Peace of Amiens in March 1802.

77   The Countess of Huntingdon had been impressed by Wesley's teaching. In 1739 she joined the first Methodist society in London and, when Whitefield and Wesley split over a question of doctrine, she took Whitefield's side and made him her personal chaplain. She opened the Countess of Huntingdon's Chapel in Bath in 1765 and was largely responsible for introducing Methodism to the upper classes.

78   TW, pp.215–224.

79   AJR, Jul 1802, vol.11, pp.306–307.

80   More to Wilberforce, spring 1802, cited in William Roberts, *Memoirs of the Life and Correspondence of Hannah More*, 3rd ed., 1838, vol.3, p.181.

81   Margaret Elton, *Annals of the Elton Family: Bristol Merchants and Somerset Landowners*, Alan Sutton Publishing Ltd 1994, p.108.

82   AJR, Aug 1802, vol.12, p.429.

83   AJR, Febr 1802, vol.11, p.194.

84   AJR, Apr 1802, vol.11, p.424.

85   AJR, Mar 1800, vol.5, p.330.

86   AJR, Apr 1802, vol.11, p.429.

87   Cited in Ford K Brown, *Fathers of the Victorians: The Age of Wilberforce*, Cambridge University Press 1961, p.216.

88   TW, p.224.

89   More to Beadon, spring 1802, cited in William Roberts, *Memoirs of the Life and Correspondence of Mrs Hannah More*, 3rd ed., vol.3, pp.123–139.

90   Beadon to More, *ibid*, pp.140–141.

91   Charles Daubeny, *Vindiciae Ecclesiae Anglicanae*, London & Bath 1803, p.23.

92   AJR, Dec 1803, vol.16, pp.531–532.

93   *Journal of John Wesley*, ed. Nehemiah Curnock, II, 31st Mar 1739, p.167, cited in Kenneth Morgan, *John Wesley in Bristol*, Bristol Branch of the Historical Association 1990.

94   TB, p.64.

95   More to Wilberforce, 2nd Sep 1800, Duke, cited in AS, p.241.

96   MM, p.226.

97   MM, p.21.

98   TW, p.179.

99   More to Wilberforce, 2nd Sep 1800, Duke, cited in AS, p.241.

100   TW, pp.224–225.

101   Emily Lorraine de Montzulin, *The Anti-Jacobins 1798-1800: The Early Contributors to the Anti-Jacobin Review*, Macmillan Press Ltd 1988, p.20.

[102] MM, p.13.

[103] Lyndall Gordon, *Mary Wollstonecraft: A New Genus*, Little Brown, 2005, p.154.

[104] The French Jacobin Club, or the Society of the Friends of the Constitution, was initially moderate and its members were professionals outside political office. It soon broadened its membership and became more radical and during the Terror became one of the most powerful political institutions in France.

[105] MM, p.63.

[106] MM, p.68.

[107] MM, pp.77-78.

[108] TW, p.16.

[109] Tom Mayberry, *Coleridge and Wordsworth in the West Country*, Alan Sutton Publishing Ltd, 1992, pp.88-99.

[110] The Society of United Irishmen was a coalition of radicals, Catholics, a few liberal aristocrats and politically sidelined professional and business classes. Organised in 1790 in support of parliamentary reform, the society quickly established close relations with radical societies in England. In 1794, after its secretary was tried for treason and fled to Paris, the society went underground and became a secret extremist group dedicated to turning Ireland into a republic by force. Its leaders were in treasonous contact with the French government leading to attempted invasions of Ireland in 1796 and 1797, followed by repression of the society. Desperation led to further insurrection in May 1798 and three more abortive French invasions.

[111] S. Andrews, 'Pitt and Anti-Jacobin Hysteria', *History Today* 48, Sep 1998, pp.49-54.

[112] AJR, vol.1, Jul 1798.

[113] John Gifford was not related to William Gifford.

[114] Emily Lorraine de Montzulin, *The Anti-Jacobins 1798-1800: The Early Contributors to the Anti-Jacobin Review*, Macmillan Press Ltd 1988, pp.25-28.

[115] AS, p.242.

[116] AS, p.242.

[117] The belief that there was a providential order in society: the ruling classes existed to govern and use their wealth for benevolence and philanthropy; merchants and farmers provided employment for the masses; and the poor provided the labour force for factories, mines, farms and the homes of the wealthy.

[118] AJR, Oct 1800, vol.7, pp.215-217.

[119] J. Sack, *From Jacobite to Conservative: Reaction and Orthodoxy in Britain c1760-1832*, Cambridge 1993, p.24.

[120] Emily Lorraine de Montzulin, *The Anti-Jacobins 1798-1800: The Early Contributors to the Anti-Jacobin Review*, Macmillan Press Ltd 1988, p.27, pp.94-96.

[121] J. Sack, *From Jacobite to Conservative: Reaction and Orthodoxy in Britain c1760-1832*, Cambridge 1993, p.14.

[122] TW, pp.188-189.
[123] Cheap Repository Tracts were little books written by the More sisters and their friends, based on personal experience, to promote good morals among the poor. Examples include *The Sunday School* and *Hester Wilmot*.
[124] Beadon to More, spring 1802, cited in William Roberts, *Memoirs of the Life and Correspondence of Hannah More*, 3rd ed., 1838, vol.3, pp.140-141.
[125] AS, p.239.
[126] Diary of Hannah More, cited in William Roberts, *Memoirs of the Life and Correspondence of Hannah More*, 3rd ed., 1838, vol.3, p.208.

Select Bibliography

Printed Primary Sources

Martha More, *Mendip Annals, or, the Narrative of the Charitable Labours of Hannah and Martha More*, ed. Arthur Roberts, London 1859.
Thomas Bere, *The Controversy between Mrs Hannah More and the Curate of Blagdon, relative to the Conduct of her Teacher of the Sunday School in that Parish,* London 1801.
Abraham Elton, *A Letter to the Rev. Thomas Bere, Rector of Butcombe, Occasioned by his Late Unwarrantable Attack on Mrs Hannah More,* London and Bath 1801. This pamphlet and others are kept in Bath and Bristol Reference Libraries.
Thomas Sedgwick Whalley, *The Journals and Correspondence of Thomas Sedgewick* [Sedgwick] *Whalley,* ed. Hill Wickham, 2 vols, London 1863.
The Anti-Jacobin Review, vols. 4, 5, 7, 9-12.

Secondary Sources

Henry Thompson, *The Life of Hannah More with Notices of her Sisters*, London 1838 .
M. G. Jones, *Hannah* More, Cambridge University Press, 1952.
Ford K. Brown, *Fathers of the Victorians: The Age of Wilberforce,* Cambridge University Press 1961, chapter 6.
Anne Stott, *Hannah More: Evangelicalism, Cultural Reformation and Loyalism,* unpublished PhD Thesis, University College London, 1998.
Anne Stott, *Hannah More: The First Victorian*, Oxford University Press 2003.
Elizabeth Harvey, *Hannah More and her connections with Blagdon: Part 1 - Early Life, relationship with Langhorne, and the Mendip Schools*, A History of Blagdon, vol.2, 2006, pp.75-96.
Margaret Elton, *Annals of the Elton Family: Bristol Merchants and Somerset Landowners,* Alan Sutton Publishing Ltd, 1994.
Kenneth Morgan, *John Wesley in Bristol*, Bristol Branch of the Historical Association 1990.

John Kent, *Wesley and the Wesleyans: Religion in Eighteenth-Century Britain*, Cambridge University Press, 2002.

J. Steven Watson, *The Reign of George III 1760-1815*, Oxford University Press, 1960.

M. J. Sydenham, *The French Revolution*, B.T. Batsford Ltd, 1965.

R. K. Webb, *Modern England: from the 18th Century to the Present*, Allen and Unwin 1980.

Lyndall Gordon, *Mary Wollstonecraft: A New Genus*, Little Brown, 2005.

Antonia Fraser, *Marie Antoinette: The Journey*, Weidenfeld & Nicholson, 2001.

Tom Mayberry, *Coleridge and Wordsworth in the West Country*, Alan Sutton Publishing Ltd, 1992.

James Gillray, *Satirical Etchings of James Gillray*.

Emily Lorraine de Montzulin, *The Anti-Jacobins 1798-1800: The Early Contributors to the Anti-Jacobin Review*, Macmillan Press Ltd 1988.

S. Andrews, 'Pitt and Anti-Jacobin Hysteria', *History Today* 48, September 1998, pp.49–54.

J. Sack, *From Jacobite to Conservative: Reaction and Orthodoxy in Britain c1760-1832*, Cambridge 1993.

The Baptist Church in Blagdon

Neil Bentham

The history of the Baptist Church dates from 1611, *'when it was founded in exile in Amsterdam by a group of Separatists from the Church of England led by John Smith'.*[1] In England, *'the first Baptist Church was formed in London in 1612'.*[2] On 3rd June 1679, *'Edward Terrill, a wealthy Bristolian and elder of the Broadmead Baptist Church, signed a deed of gift in favour of his church. It was to be used after his death for the support of a minister at Broadmead ... whose chief task would be that of preparing young men for ministry among the Baptist churches of the land.'*[3] *'The Baptist Union was formed in 1813 and by 1824 there was a thrust towards expansion and evangelism'.*[4]

However, as far as Blagdon is concerned, the oldest dissenters' record in the BLHS archive is a request (known as a Protestant Dissenters Certificate) to the Bishop of Bath and Wells, dated December 30th 1776, to license a dwelling in Blagdon for divine worship (fig. 1).

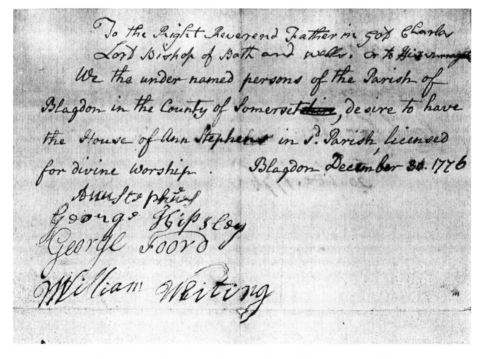

Fig. 1 – Dissenters certificate dated December 30th 1776 (copy in BLHS archives)

The certificate states:

To the Right Reverend Father in God Charles Lord Bishop of Bath and Wells, we the under named persons of the Parish of Blagdon in the County of Somerset, desire to have the House of Ann Stephens in the Parish licensed for Divine Worship. Blagdon, December 30 1776

> *Ann Stephens*
> *George Hipsley*
> *George Foord*
> *William Whiting* [5]

Protestant Dissenters Certificates had their origin in the Act of Toleration, passed by the English Parliament on 24th May 1689 with the stated aim of *'Exempting their Majestyes Protestant Subjects dissenting from the Church of England from the Penalties of certaine Lawes'*. The Act granted freedom of worship to Nonconformists – that is those Protestants who dissented from the Church of England such as Baptists, Congregationalists, and Quakers, but not Catholics. The Act allowed Nonconformists their own places of worship and their own preachers, subject to the acceptance of certain oaths of allegiance. The exclusion of Catholics and Unitarians continued the existing social and political disabilities for any proclaimed dissenters, including their exclusion from political office. Fifty years later the Methodists were similarly affected when, in 1740, the Methodist Society was founded.

The practical administration of the Act of Toleration required that a group of dissenters had to apply to the Bishop for a licence and be registered, if they wished to establish a house or chapel to be used for divine worship within the Diocese. It has also to be recognised that the Church of England, prior to the Reformation in 1534, worshipped in accordance with the rites and rituals of the Catholic Church with services spoken and read in Latin. Since some rural congregations could not even read or write in English, it must have been difficult, if not impossible, for the uneducated rural peasant to follow the Church service in Latin. The Nonconformists had no such linguistic liturgical problems.

The request of 1776 is one of the ten records of registration, variously dated 1776, 1795, 1796, 1805, 1808, 1813, and 1817, covering properties in Blagdon, Charterhouse, Rickford and Wrington. Copies are held in the BLHS archive. Out of the ten applications, seven are for houses, one is for an outhouse or warehouse and two are for chapels. Of the two chapels, the oldest is described as, '… *the Chapel lately erected in the town and Parish of Wrington … certificate granted 30 January 1796.'* The second request is for a chapel already built in Blagdon, dated 19th November 1808, which states:

'To the Right Reverend Lord Bishop of Bath and Wells
We the undersigned being part of a congregation of Protestant Dissenters from
the Church of England have lately erected a building or Chapel for Divine Worship
in the Parish of Blagdon in your Lordship's Diocese. We beg the said Building or
Chapel to be Licensed and registered accordingly.

> *James Davis*
> *Charles Edward Rawlins*
> *William Gallop*
> *George Caple*
> *John Lawrence*
> *James Cross*
> *James Caple*
> *James Fear'* [6]

Although no denomination is stated, it is not unreasonable to infer that it was a Baptist chapel because three years earlier, on 6th August 1805, an application had been sent to the Bishop on behalf of the Methodists. This will be referred to in the article on the history of Methodism in Blagdon.[7]

One of the difficulties in relating these Protestant Dissenters applications to register or license a house or a chapel to a particular building is that the property is identified by a list of the names of the dissenters rather than by the address or location of the property to be registered – presumably because there were relatively few residents and everybody would have known where somebody lived. The significance of this will become apparent later.

In 1776 in a village such as Blagdon there were fewer houses and even fewer chapels than we see today, although *'the Wesleys (1703-1791) began the Methodist Movement in 1738, with the Methodist Society founded in 1740'.*[8] The Tithe Map of 1842, over a century later, in addition to identifying and numbering the fields and parcels of land, also showed buildings (fig. 6). The map shows that, within a hundred yards of the Blagdon turnpike toll house (now demolished but sited at the important junction of the Butcombe road, now Station Road, and the Bath road, now High Street), were clustered, at the most, some twenty houses. This location is typical for such groupings, another being significant river crossings that also attracted embryonic settlement development.[9]

The Dissenters application of 1808 raises a question. If the 1805 application can be regarded as relating to the Primitive Methodist chapel (the cottage that we now know as Chapel Grove Court, overlooking the A368 Bath Road) – and the records of the Methodist Church kept by Mrs Jean Darby of Congresbury give a date of

1807 for the building of this chapel at a cost of £400 – where was the Baptist chapel that was built and occupied shortly before 1808?

Before attempting to suggest a possible answer, it is necessary to try to understand the subsequent events that occurred as the Protestant Dissenters movement began to grow and develop, in response to the influence generated by the founders of the Baptist Church and other leading evangelical preachers of the time. That growth was marked by the ability of the faithful, over time, to generate sufficient donations and gifts to gradually move from holding their early religious services in their own cottages to acquiring land and buildings for a purpose-built chapel, as a plain but recognisable architectural building type. The use of houses by the early dissenters is in keeping with the earliest notion of collective worship among Christians when Jesus said, *'For where two or three are gathered together in my name, there am I in the midst of them.'*[10]

On 18th December 1813 the Dissenters records contain an application by *'William Jefferis who sought permission from the Bishop of Bath and Wells to use his house, at Charterhouse in the Parish of Blagdon, as a place of religious worship'.*[11]

On 5th July 1817 approval was granted to an application made to the Lord Bishop of Bath and Wells by Joseph Hind Browning and five other dissenters to use, *'an outhouse or warehouse belonging to Mr William Panes of Blagdon … as a place of Religious Worship'.*[12]

On 13th February 1828, *'I John Williams, of the Parish of Blagdon … do hereby certify that a dwelling house in my possession in the village of Rickford in the parish and County aforesaid … is intended to be used as a place of religious worship by an Assembly or Congregation of Protestants…'.*[13]

However, there is now a significant gap in the records of some 47 years before the thread of history of the Baptist Church in Blagdon can be picked up again, based upon the handwritten entries in the four small ledgers that have survived since the earliest account was written down in 1875. The account refers to events in about 1850, some 25 years earlier, that happened in Blagdon's western parish boundary district of Rickford.

Although there are gaps, enough of the records survive to convey a sense of the faith that motivated those early Baptists in their desire to promote their Christian beliefs in Blagdon. The Rickford records begin with John Williams (1828) and the others who came after him.

Therefore from 1776, when the first recorded house in Blagdon was used for divine worship, it was to take another 32 years until 1808 before the first written record of a chapel having been built is recognised. But where was this new chapel? Has any fragment of the building survived? Why has nobody else mentioned a newly built chapel? It must have been a significant event in the life of the early Baptist Church. Apart from that one single page application to the Bishop, held in the archives of the Somerset Record Office (a copy is in the BLHS archive), it has not even been hinted at in the surviving records. Do the missing Baptist Church records contain the clue? Until those missing records turn up, or some other evidence comes to light, we are faced with an enigma.

However, 37 years later, in 1845, there is an eyewitness account of a visit to Blagdon, and I shall refer to that and the existence of an oddly tall building that has been in almost continuous use, but whose original purpose has never been satisfactorily explained, in due course.

The oldest of the surviving Blagdon Baptist Church ledgers (which I have called Vol.1) is handwritten in the copperplate style of the times, and records events as follows:

'About the year of one thousand eight hundred and fifty some of the Preachers of the Bristol Baptist Itinerant Society visited Blagdon and commenced to conduct services which were the means of great spiritual blessing to many persons – in an upper room – the club room, of a house once known as the, 'Old Bell' the services were thus conducted every Lord's day evening until September 6th 1875 on which day our Chapel was opened and named the 'Jubilee Chapel' it having been built to commemorate the Jubilee of the Bristol Baptists Itinerant Society'.[14]

Amongst the papers in the BLHS 'Dissenters' archive file is a handwritten note by Kathleen Rose Jones (née Gallop), who lived in Clennon House, that says:

'In 1850 a request from believers in Blagdon was sent to the Bristol Baptist Society, to organise regular services in the village. The Club Room of the Old Bell Inn was hired and Worship was continued there every Sunday for the next 25 years. Often the room was very crowded, and it was approached by an outside flight of 26 stone steps. It was very low, and farmer William Derrick (My great grandfather) very awkward, as he stood to give out the hymns, with a request to his daughter (my grandmother) to 'pitch the tune Polly.'

'In 1871, land was secured to build a new Chapel and the members were anxious to, 'arise and build'. A request was made to their liberal-minded friends in Bristol to come to Blagdon to help raise funds to erect their much needed House of Prayer, as their own members were unable to find the estimated cost of £300, due to their numbers and social position'.[15]

At some time after the Ordnance Survey Somerset Sheet XV111.7 edition of 1931 was published showing the Bell Inn still in existence it was partially demolished, but the blocked outlines of some of its windows and door openings can still be seen in the north-facing stone wall that forms a part of the boundary walls to the south side of Bell Square off Station Road and the property now known as 'Old Bell House' (fig. 2).

Fig. 2 – The north facing wall of the Bell Inn. The outline of the original doorways and windows may still be seen. (author's photograph)

The reported 25 year use of the upper floor of the Bell Inn also omits any mention of the Baptists ritual of baptism by total immersion, and in what way that defining ritual was arranged within such limited facilities.

The Blagdon Church records confirm and continue the story to the eventual building and opening of the new Blagdon Jubilee Chapel on 6th September 1875 (fig. 3), as outlined below;

'*The Rev. E. G. Gange, Minister of Broadmead Baptist Chapel Bristol preached the opening Sermon in the afternoon to an overflowing congregation from the 2nd Chapter of the Epistle to the Philippians and the 16th Verse.*

'*After the service a tea-meeting took place, in a tent in a field kindly lent by Capt. Newnham, and some six hundred persons sat down to tea. After the tables were cleared a Public Meeting was held and presided over by George Hare Leonard Esq., the Treasurer Mr George M. Carlile read the financial account★ Addresses were given by the Rev. J. Perry, Minister of Buckingham Chapel Clifton, Rev. J.D. Evans, minister of Old King Street Baptist Chapel, W. J. Mayers, Minister of City Road Baptist Chapel, E. J. Grange and George C. Ashmead Esq. of Clifton.*
It was a day of great gladness and we said, 'The Lord has done great things for us whereof we are glad'. [16]

The financial account read by Mr George M. Carlile, provides a long list of donations and also the costs incurred in building the new Jubilee Chapel in what is now known as Mead Lane off the High Street:

	$£$	s.	d.	
To Purchase of Ground –	*95*	*0*	*0*	
.. Building the Chapel as per				
Mr J. Clark's contract -	*476*	*0*	*0*	
.. Trust and Conveyance Deed-	*8*	*16*	*0*	
.. Mr Challenger for early				
possession of Ground.-	*3*	*10*	*0*	
	£583	*6*	*0*	[17]

★An amount that exactly matched the donations referred to above.

*Fig. 3 – Blagdon Baptist Jubilee chapel built by John Clark in 1875
(photographs Sheila Johnson and author)*

It appears that the friendly relationship and mutual support that existed between the Rickford Baptists and those in Blagdon may be judged by the next entry, some eight weeks later, in the Blagdon Church ledger (Vol. 1) as follows:

On Sunday October 31st 1875 the following friends were formed into a Church by Mr M. J. Thomas (who also became their Pastor) all of them having been members of the Baptist Church at Rickford from which they were honourably dismissed and commended to each others confidence by a letter then read.
Mr. William Bodey and Mr. J. Swaish preachers of the Bristol Baptist Itinerant Society then addressed the newly formed Church.

Charles Derrick   *Mrs. M. Carpenter*
Mrs. M .A .Gallop   *Mrs. John Pikex[18]*

A printed report from the Bristol Baptist Itinerant Society has been cut out from a larger report and pasted into the Blagdon Church ledger, from which the following extract is taken:

'Your Committee are thankful to hear that the Chapel is crowded every Sunday evening. A Church has been formed, and the little band held their first communion on the last Sunday in October. Two believers are waiting for baptism; and Mr. Thomas has reason to believe that there are some secret disciples in the congregation, and hopes they will soon make a profession of their faith. A Sabbath School has also been commenced, and the attendance thereat is between thirty and forty. Thus the desire of many years has been gratified by the erection of the Chapel, and the results so far have been highly encouraging'.[19]

The events of the Church are recorded as they occur and this short essay does not attempt to repeat them all as the months and years pass by. However, the author has selected extracts that appear to have significance in helping us, 132 years later, to better understand how the organisation of the church and its growth and development flourished in the tradition of the dissenters.

The Church Meeting held on November 28th 1875 records:

Resolved that a letter should be sent to Mr G. M. Carlile through whose efforts under God we mainly owe the erection of our Chapel to thank him for the same, also that a letter be sent to Mr & Mrs Merrick to thank them for their kind gifts of a cushion for the reading desk and a plated Communion service, the pastor provided ...

Church Meeting March 26th 1876. *Resolved that Mr. & Mrs. G. Clark, be received for Baptism and Membership and the first Baptismal service to be held on Sunday April 28th 1876.*

April 28th 1876. *The Pastor preached and Mr G.M. Carlile baptized Mr & Mrs G. Clark and at the Communion Service the Pastor gave them the right hand of fellowship.*[20]

The transfer of dissenters from one chapel to another was a matter of importance to the overall organisation and administration of the Church and from the ledger it is possible to gain some idea of this 'exchange' practice both to and from our neighbouring villages. Examples of these transfers are as follows:

Church Meeting November 28th 1875
Received into fellowship by letter Mr and Mrs Edgil from the Baptist Church at Ridgehill.[21]

Church Meeting December 31st 1876
Resolved to apply to the Church at Charterhouse for the transfer of Mrs J. Brunt from their fellowship to ours.[22]

Church Meeting January 28th 1877
A letter from Mr Luke Boyce in connection with the Plymouth Brethren Church at Charterhouse was read commending Mrs J. Brunt to our fellowship. Resolved to receive Mrs J. Brunt to our Membership. Resolved to apply for the transfer of Mr M. Weaver from the Baptist Church at Ridgehill.[23]

Almost a year later, on **30th December 1877**, the record states that, *'Blagdon had received a request from the Baptist Church at Wickwar to send them a letter transferring our brother M. Weaver to their fellowship, he having in the providence of God gone to reside at Wickwar – resolved that a letter of transfer be sent'.*[24]

Church Meeting August 26th 1877
Mr J. Brunt received the right hand of fellowship he having been previously baptised.[25]

Church Meeting September 30th 1877
Resolved to apply to the Baptist Church at Counterslip Chapel Bristol for the transfer of Mr & Mrs George Wescott.[26]

It was noted earlier that in October 1875 a Sunday School was commenced with between thirty and forty children attending. The printed reports about the Blagdon Baptists, cut out and pasted into the church ledger and noted as, '...*extracted from the B.B.I. Society's report for 1883 or 59th Report'*, and '*extracted from the Bristol Western Daily Press for May 8th 1884'*, present a glowing account of the building and opening of the new Sunday School that had been built behind the Chapel. The article also confirmed that Mr C. Merrick was to be the settled pastor of the Church which was an experiment tried by the Bristol Baptist Itinerant Society whose preachers had, for many years, visited the village and held services every Sunday.

'*The pastor, Mr Merrick had designed the building and the builder was Mr Clark from Rickford. It was reported that the Sunday school would accommodate 150 to 180 children and had all the conveniences for carrying on teaching in classes.*

'*The costs for the building were stated as £210, the cost of benches £16 13s but to this had to be added two or three small extras amounting to about £10 so the total costs would be £236 13s. Mr Merrick was reported as saying he had received, or been promised, sums amounting to £180 19s. These sums included £53 16s 3d voted by the Itinerant Society, £30 from Mr W. H. Wills, M.P., £25 from Mr & Mrs Carlile, and £5 from the chairman. A balance of £53 13s 11d was still required to free the building from debt. There were more than 100 scholars on the books, an increase of 25 in the year.*

'*It was pointed out in the report that in 1831 the population of Blagdon was 1,111; 50 years later in 1881 the population was 909, a reduction of 202 – in contrast the population of Bristol had doubled. Mr Carlile also expressed delight that the days when they had held their services in the Bell Inn Club Room had passed and they now had, for such a village as this, a commodious and, he ventured to say, a very pretty place of worship*'.[27]

For the benefit of a stranger to the area reading this account, Rickford is a small hamlet of about 100 souls (2000 AD)[28], about one mile west of the main village of Blagdon, that sits astride the parish boundary between Blagdon and Burrington. The boundary is marked, at this point, by a powerful stream that rises as a natural spring on the south side of the main road (A368) that runs roughly east and west and joins Bath, 21 miles to the east, to Weston-super-Mare on the coast of the Bristol Channel, twelve miles to the west.

The spring produces some three million gallons of water a day (13.7 million litres). The stream is referred to in a Saxon charter of 904 relating to the Manor of Wrington as, 'the large spring of Schirebourne'[29], and defines a part of the western parish boundary. For over a thousand years, that part of Rickford which occupies the north-eastern bank of the stream was a part of Blagdon, with the western bank in the Parish of Burrington. Rickford is not mentioned in the Domesday Book since it was a part of Blagdon. Aldwick defined the northern extremity of Blagdon parish and Charterhouse marks the southern extremity. The eastern parish boundary with Ubley is just to the east of Merecombe Farm and follows the line of the Ubley Drove Road up onto the plateau of Mendip.

The Rickford stream not only provided a boundary marker, it also provided the Baptists of Rickford with a baptismal focus central to their beliefs, that is still present, *'in a small flight of stone steps leading down to the water from the lawn of Mill house'* [30] (Fig. 4), for the total immersion of the baptismal candidates.

Fig. 4 – Mill House, Rickford
(author's photograph)

Baptismal steps, the only evidence that survives of the earlier Baptist chapel that was demolished along with the mill.

The Baptists of Rickford must have been a hardy lot to withstand the sudden immersion of baptism in the cold, clear waters of the Schirebourne stream. The research by the Rickford History Group published in the millennium year 2000 has provided a fascinating insight into some of the earliest recorded beginnings of the Baptists in Blagdon.

The reflections in the still clear waters of Rickford Pond of a striking red and white, steeply pitched roofed, church-like building, with a tower and an external covered but open staircase, almost in the idiom of some wayward folly, often causes the passing tourist to make a hasty stop in order to photograph this slightly surreal building that marks Rickford as nothing else does (fig. 5)

Fig. 5 – Rickford chapel c1911
(Duncan Day collection BLHS Archives)

The building was commissioned by W.H. Wills as a Baptist chapel and hall and was completed in 1888. There had been an earlier Baptist chapel close by, along with a barn, yard, mill and cottages, and these were all bought by W.H. Wills in 1885 [*see Appendix 1*] and demolished to make way for the new chapel.[31] The chapel served the Baptists of Rickford for the next 75 years until in 1963 the church's use came to an end and the chapel was taken over by the new Forest of Mendip Masonic Lodge.

The Rickford research states that, *'It seems that a number of dissenters lived in Rickford in the early part of the 19th century … Deeds of Dissent were signed by the Bishop of Bath and Wells registering dwellings in Rickford to be used, 'as a place of religious worship by an Assembly or Congregation of Protestants.'* Also, the Chapel mentioned above was originally operated by the Methodists until 1854, when the work was taken over by the Baptists. The chapel apparently stood in a courtyard, and a good congregation would often gather for services. An 'open' church was eventually formed in 1859, and the former Methodist attendants were allowed to join. Contention arose, however, because the Methodists were not baptised, and they subsequently resigned.[32]

The itinerant nature of the Baptist church ministry has already been mentioned, but an interested observer began to publish accounts of his church-going, anonymously, in the *Bristol Times* between 1843 and 1845. The articles were eventually gathered together and re-published in three small volumes. Volume 2 was published in 1850, under the title, *The Church Goer: Rural Rides or calls at Country Churches (Second Series)*. The writer was subsequently revealed as Joseph Leech, who was born on 19th March 1815 and died, at the age of 78, on 13th August 1893. It was his custom to set out on Sunday mornings and visit either city churches or rural churches. Early in the morning of 20th July 1845, he set off from Bristol on his horse John Bunyan heading for St Andrews Blagdon and the morning service. In the afternoon he walked north, down the hill from Blagdon, across the tiny bridge that spanned the small stream of the River Yeo, and along Blagdon Lane into the village of Butcombe to visit St Michael and All Angels for Evensong. His opinions and somewhat acidic comments on what he saw make interesting reading, especially so in regard to the enigma mentioned earlier.

However, Joseph Leech's eye-witness experience on the first part of his journey to Blagdon tells us about the training regime required of the students attending the Baptist Training College in Bristol. I quote his comments in full:

Blagdon

As I rode through Bedminster on the morning of my visit to Blagdon, a kind of Cobourg (I think you call it), or market-cart, in which were a number of young men with black coats and white neckcloths, passed me; and soon after pulled up and deposited one of its semi-clerical-looking company in front of something like a conventicle. The conveyance then proceeded on its way; and as I was curious enough to wish to know what this meant, I pushed John to 'a prettier pace' and was enabled to keep up with it, until another black coat and white neckcloth popped out near Bishport; the Cobourg still continuing its course, and, doubtless, dispensing more young ministers, like a shower of manna, by the way. This, I afterwards learned, was a conveyance belonging to the Baptist College in Stoke's Croft, from which it starts every Sunday morning for the country, with a cargo of young students, who are dropt in the manner referred to along a given line, and amongst congregations who are waiting their advent. The Cobourg having conveyed the ' last man' to the remotest chapel, waits until he has preached; and then, retracing its road, picks up the others in its progress, after they have got rid of their pent-up orations also. This is, doubtless, a good plan for young men to try their nascent theology and rhetoric on rural audiences; but, without wishing to say anything disrespectful of the College or the students (who are also named on such occasions 'supplies') the return career of the Cobourg resembled, in my imagination, calling for empty cans, inasmuch as each young man had by this time discharged himself of his discourse.

Blagdon is a long ride from Bristol, but a beautiful one; and I should have had a fellow-traveller through Rickford Combe and the Vale of Burrington, for it is barren work riding amid the most picturesque scenery, and having nobody by your side to whom to say, 'How beautiful!' My only companionship was the drowsy creaking of John's saddle and the singing of the birds. In the olden time, before the age of rails, I must have met, by Redhill and along the road, some Exeter coach; but as I passed the Inn at the former place, which was once so famous for egg-flip, as the passenger on the Estafette was possibly well aware, I could not help comforting myself with the reflection, that there was something more lone than a solitary horseman – and that was, a way-side inn after a railroad had run away with its customers.

On arriving at the toll-bar at Blagdon, I pulled out my penny to pay for John. 'It is double 'pike to-day Sir,' said the man in charge.
'Indeed,' said I, 'are not people allowed to pass free to Church?'
'Yes Sir, but they be the parishioners.'
'And how do you know friend that my residence is not within your boundaries?', I enquired.
The man looked at me archly, as he answered, 'You could not be in the parish and people not know it. If you staid at home, you'd have nothing to pay.'
'There, my worthy neighbour,' said I, giving him the two-pence; 'it is well if a double 'pike be the only penalty I shall have to pay for my Sunday vagrancy.'

Whether it was that they were looking out for 'a supply' or not, I can't say; but most of the congregation of the sole Dissenting chapel at Blagdon were standing in front of the building, and seemingly on the watch for somebody. For a moment I was apprehensive that they might have taken me and John for what we were not, as they made rather a critical survey of both; so to prevent mistakes, I took refuge in the Seymour Arms, and having housed the quadruped, I proceeded along a very prettily kept pathway through the fields to the Church, from and about which there is one of the noblest and most extensive prospects I think I have ever seen, at least in Somersetshire. From the churchyard, as if from a platform, you look down on a vast vale, and right across to Redhill and Wrington, catching in your cursory glance the gabled roof of many an English residence, rising amidst its 'tall ancestral trees'. Hard by was a little clear spring, in which, as the day was sultry, I bathed my hands, and fancied that many a mendicant friar had done the same in the same spot before me.[33]

The above eyewitness account of a visit to Blagdon illuminates the enigma, which is this. When, on 20th July 1845, Joseph Leech saw, '... *most of the congregation of the sole dissenting chapel at Blagdon were standing in front of the building, and seemingly on the watch for somebody ...'*, which building were they standing in front of that would have been clearly visible to John Leech as he paid his toll at the turnpike house?

Since the Baptist Chapel in Mead Lane wasn't built until thirty years later in 1875 the congregation could not have been standing in front of that building watching Joseph Leech astride his horse paying his 'Double Pike' at the toll gate!

It is equally unlikely that the congregation were standing outside the Bell Inn in Bell Square, because that was a pub, and the Baptists only used the top floor club room. In any event, the toll gate was about 100 yards from the site of the Bell Inn and is out of direct line of sight due to the bend in the Butcombe Road (renamed Station Road after the railway opened in Blagdon on 4th December 1901).

This obviously leaves us repeating the question, where was this, '... *sole Dissenting Chapel'* that was built before the Bishop of Bath and Wells was asked to, '*Licence and Register the same'* on 19th November 1808?

In an effort to make plain the elements of this enigma thus far we have, firstly, the dissenters' request to the Bishop in November 1808 (when Britain was still at war with France[34]). Secondly, there is Joseph Leech's eyewitness account of the congregation standing outside the sole Dissenting Chapel on 20th July 1845. (Two years earlier, in 1843, Isambard Kingdom Brunel had launched the largest ship in the world, the SS Great Britain, in Bristol Docks,[35] and in the 1844 potato famine was starting in Ireland.[36]) Thirdly, are there any remains still standing of the chapel that was built in 1808, and, if so, why has nobody been able to identify them during the last 199 years? Has the slate of living memory been wiped clean? It is odd that nothing has survived, no drawing, map or artefact, nor a record written of this chapel.

There is also another question at present unanswered, which is, since this chapel did exist, why did it stop being used after a period of 42 years (1808-1850) and the top floor of the Bell Inn, up 26 steps and with a ceiling so low a tall farmer had difficulty standing upright to conduct the services, become the preferred meeting place − for the next 25 years?

Perhaps we should begin to look for some answers in what lies about us. In the introductory article − *Blagdon Local History Society: the beginning* − in Volume 1 of *A History of Blagdon* (2004) it was stated that, '*The first known use of Court Lodge was as a cottage next door to the Turnpike Toll House and shown on the Tithe Map of 1842 ...'(Fig*

6). The introduction goes on to state, '*The lower two-room semi-basement level had been abandoned due to dampness for many years, but the building work revealed its cottage origins, and due to its close proximity to Blagdon's Tollhouse, provided some clues as to the original level of the turnpike highway some 200 years earlier.*'

During the survey of the property prior to the design work other facts came to light. The remains of a staircase that had been eaten away by woodworm – to the extent that it had, at some time during the last two hundred years, quietly collapsed in the darkness of the unused basement. But the remains of the worm-eaten staircase implied an upper floor at some time in the past. The west elevation that is facing on to the High Street contained, at its south end, the blocked in outlines of two small windows and a door, also a blocked inglenook – although the chimneys had long since been removed above roof level. One window and a very low door – the only access into the basement – along with the remains of a wash boiler set in a brick plinth, with an open floor drain, were in the northern end room of the basement. The height of the entire basement at 7ft 2½in (2.2m) was consistent with the typical vernacular domestic scale of other similar 200 year old cottages elsewhere in the village. Originally, it is likely that the cottage would have had a first floor, perhaps within a steeply pitched thatched roof that inclined to a central ridge from some 3 or 4 feet (1–1.6m) above the present upper floor level. Again, this is a construction technique consistent with the low social rural status of many of the cottages in the village, but we do not know with certainty.

However what is known, that was revealed during the survey of the cottage, is that its first floor, presumed a thatched roof structure, had been removed at some time in the past, and its outer first floor walls extended upwards to the considerable height of 10ft 3in (3.1m) internally – which is some 3 or 4ft above bedroom height in a typical vernacular cottage.

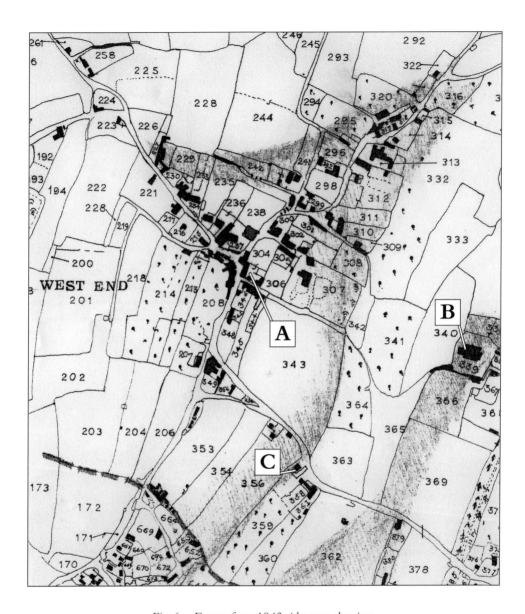

Fig. 6 – Extract from 1842 tithe map showing:

(A) Court Lodge, presumed site of Baptist chapel and adjacent stable
(B) St Andrew's church
(C) The early Methodist chapel

Several of the traditional cottages in Blagdon have had their eaves levels raised, and their roof pitches flattened, in order to meet the 20th century demands of the building regulations on the one hand and planning policy on the other, but none so high as to cater for giants! So why the great height, and why the much taller and wider first floor windows – five of them at first floor level?

A study of the science of building types perhaps provides a clue. It is an oft-quoted tenet in issues of architectural design theory that 'form follows function': in other words, in the best buildings their designs have their genesis in their function. The cathedral, as an example, is a majestic, soaring, awe-inspiring edifice that induces a feeling of reverence, provides a sense of the sublime, excels in visual patterns of light and shade, is a revelation in structural brilliance, echoes with the cadences of sound, in voice, chime, pipe and bell, that overwhelm us and lift our spirits. The pulpit high to one side, the altar table central, to administer the Holy Sacrament, the Bishop's throne, even unoccupied, a symbol of divine power, of authority, of God's representative on earth, to lighten our darkness, to bless our marriages, to baptise our children, to pray for our souls, to reverently bury us at the end of our days, and as a witness to a thousand ages past and still to come.

In contrast, the plain, lowly rural chapel has the same function but its built ambience is much simpler, although no less holy in its visual message. The word, spoken from the central pulpit, is all. It does not echo in a vast space, but our focus on the preacher has no distractions. The communion is quiet, dignified and the centre of the service. The flowers on the table bring a scent of the miraculous. The walls, usually unadorned, receive the benediction of the morning sun slanting through the greenish glass. An arch is illuminated with a text, in gothic script. The hymns, in Bodoni Bold typeface arrayed in a mahogany frame, order our singing. The roof, not high but plain, reassures by Victorian simplicity the product of a gifted craftsman. There is no Rood Screen, nothing separates us from our God, no height nor depth denies our welcome. The offerings of a small body of believers who saved and built it, entire, within a year or so, complete with pitch pine pews whose ends have polished brass hoops to hold our umbrellas soaked with rain that drips silently into an enamel dish and soundlessly evaporates. The inspiration is no less magnificent, but on a lower key. The aspiration and sincerity just as profound, the same God to be obeyed, the same sins to be forgiven, the same duties of humility and obedience to be followed, the same morality to be sought after, the same confession to be offered, and the same forgiveness to be received; but in a building that became as obvious in its built form, as the mediaeval cathedral was with all its flying buttresses, towering spires and centuries of time. The same assurances from chapel and cathedral, the same faith, the same continuing witness to eternity, the same certainty, whether we listen or not to the same promise, *'And be assured, I am with you always, to the end of time'*.[37]

It is at first difficult to realise that the once-thatched cottage still stands, albeit changed beyond recognition, alongside the site of Blagdon's turnpike toll house that used to have two gates, one across the Butcombe Road and the other across the Bath Road. The same cottage now had a new higher first floor, with three large windows overlooking the High Street, topped with a new hipped roof so that it looked like a Dissenters' chapel that needed only the Bishop's imprimatur on the certificate to commence holding religious services in 1808. Where else could Joseph Leech, 37 years later in 1845, have paid his 'double pike' watched by the congregation of Blagdon's sole Dissenting chapel, itself overlooked, from further up the High Street by the Seymour Arms, where the horseman went afterwards to 'house the quadruped'. It no longer looked like a cottage, it was now too high, but it was clearly recognisable to Joseph Leech as a Dissenting chapel (figs. 7, 8).

I suggest that, based upon the evidence outlined above, the former cottage we know as Court Lodge was converted at first floor level into Blagdon's first Baptist chapel in 1808. Its outer walls were raised up, in the prevailing style, to make room for a 30-strong congregation which would need the natural light from its new, tall, larger style windows. Around the back was an entrance door, steps and porch. On the tithe map (Fig. 6 A) is a tiny square that was probably a stable for the preacher's horse, where the west end of Beech Cottage now stands, and you may still see, if you sight along the cottage wall, a slight kink that marks the end of that stable. The chapel had a new pitched and hip-ended tiled roof, with a fireplace and chimney at each end, for the chapel keeper to light and give a warm welcome on a cold winter's day.

The lower ground floor remained for a time as the original cottage, occupied by Olga Shotton's great grand-parents from about 1894 (they died before Olga was born). The architectural style of the building echoes other Baptist chapels – compare, for example, a photograph of Winford's chapel, circa 1824 (fig. 9), smaller, with only two windows, but note the proportion and height of the windows and walls and their similarity to Court Lodge.

Note also Ridgehill's former Baptist chapel, now a house, with three arched windows facing the road (fig. 10). Nempnett Thrubwell's tiny chapel (fig. 11) is no longer used as such but one can recognise the similarity of the building type in this part of rural Somerset.

Fig. 7 – High Street Blagdon. On the left is what is thought to be the original Baptist Chapel.
Taylor's Stores is in the background (George Symes collection)

Fig. 8 - Court Lodge August 2007 (author's photograph)

Fig. 9 – Winford Baptist chapel (author's photograph)

Fig. 10 – Ridgehill former Baptist chapel (author's photograph)

Fig. 11 – Nempnett Thrubwell former chapel (author's photograph)

The enigma however is not wholly dispelled because, for some reason unknown to us at present, and after 42 years, Court Lodge appears to have stopped being used as a chapel. What was the reason in 1850, five years after Joseph Leech's visit in 1845, that caused the Blagdon Baptists to leave their comfortable chapel and start climbing up 26 steps to worship in the low-ceilinged upper floor of the Bell Inn? Could there have been a fire in the chapel? It would be very helpful if we could find out what happened and why.

Court Lodge appears to have had many different uses during the last 200 years: cottage, chapel, café, Home Guard HQ, doctors' surgery – for a while it lay empty and unused, and it is now the HQ of Blagdon Local History Society.

Because we lack conclusive proof that the events described are true, we can only rely on the circumstantial evidence outlined above. It would be interesting to have the theory replaced with the historical facts, but at least the theory may perhaps encourage someone to send us some conclusive proof that can be published in the future. There is still much more to tell of the history of the Baptists in Blagdon, but that will have to wait for a future volume.

RICKFORD & NEMPNETT,

SOMERSET.

PLAN & PARTICULARS *and*
conditions of sale
OF

VALUABLE

FREEHOLD MILL,

DWELLING-HOUSE,

CHAPEL, COTTAGES,

CLOSES OF PRODUCTIVE

ORCHARD AND PASTURE LAND,

SITUATE IN THE

PARISHES OF BLAGDON & NEMPNETT, SOMERSET,

FOR

SALE BY AUCTION,

direction of the Trustees of the Will of Mr. James King, deceased,

BY

MESSRS.

GEORGE NICHOLS, SON & ALDER

AT THE

SEYMOUR ARMS HOTEL, BLAGDON,

ON

WEDNESDAY, August 5th, 1885,

At FIVE for SIX in the Evening.

Messrs. FOX & WHITTUCK,

Solicitors.

KEYNSHAM, and 35, CORN STREET, BRISTOL.

T. D. Taylor, Son, & Hawkins, Printers, "Times & Mirror" Office, Bristol.

Particulars relating to the sale of Rickford Chapel August 1885
(David Lock collection BLHS Archives)

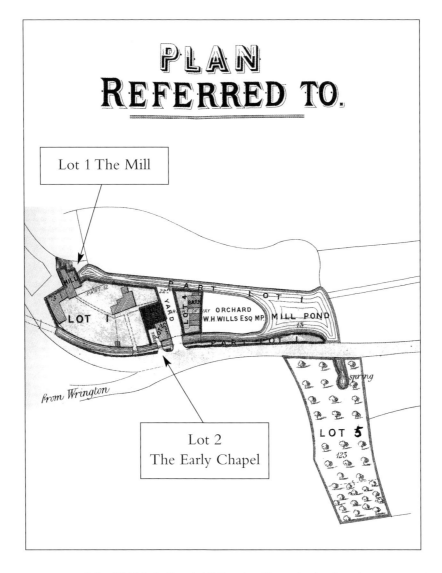

Sale of Rickford Chapel 1885 - plan illustrating lots for sale
(David Lock collection, BLHS Archives)

Acknowledgements

My thanks are due to: Barbara and Philip Hasell for arranging to make the Church Records available to me, Jean and Alec Sampson who passed on all sorts of snippets of information about the contribution made by their parents, Sammy and Ann Sampson; Peter Church, Pastor, who kindly read my draft essay; Olga Shotton for information from her family and considerable archival research in the Somerset Record Office; Sheila Johnson, who passed on innumerable sources in connection with the early Baptist Church; the staff of Bristol Central Library and in particular the Reference Library, who patiently retrieved obscure books for me; the staff of the Mobile Library; the County Record Offices at Taunton and Bristol; the out-reach Archivist Jane de Gruchy; Mrs Jean Darby of Congresbury for information on the Primitive Methodists; Mary Coward and the Rickford History Group and to the Rev. Dr Derek Teague who, as ever, found what I was looking for.

Notes and References

Bibliography

Primary Sources

The four, small notebooks, handwritten in the copperplate style of the time, record the events and decisions taken by the Church (with, confusingly, some non-sequential gaps) over the following time scales:

Volume 1 covers 50 years from 1850 to June 22nd 1900. The volume also contains the Church rolls from 31st October 1875 to 13th December 1886 and from 7th April 1891 to 25th March 1894. Names are recorded, and when and how received, including a number and remarks. Some three pages have been cut out.

Volume 2 contains Church Rules 1 to 10 dated January 1885, and covers ten years. Minutes of the Annual Church Meetings start on January 22nd 1900 and contain names and offices holders. The last entry is 14th May 1910. A church roll is included from 31st October 1875 to September 1907, a period of 32 years. (The binding of this volume is fragile and the covers loosely sellotaped together over the spine).

Volume 3 begins with the Anniversary, June 1913, lists sundry catering details and expenses, including expenses for the Anniversary July 23rd or 26th 1916. Sets out the 'Conditions for the Guidance of the Chapel Keeper', such as, *'Fire to be lighted on Sundays and when necessary'*. The Rules, dated January 1912, are restated. Church roll revised January 1912, but starts with Mr & Mrs Ash, 21st December 1886 to September 15th 1929 – 43 years. The events of the Church are recorded from January 24th 1912 to 11th July 1945, a period of 32 years.

Volume 4. Gold lettering on the spine states, Minute Book. After a 17 year gap, it contains a record of events starting with the Annual Church Meeting, March 28th 1962, and ends with, 'A Short Church Meeting was held on Tuesday September 5th 1990, signed by M.E. Higgins 9/10/90', a period of 28 years. Also contained within the record are financial notes.

Also a part of the Church records are incomplete sets of *The Blagdon Baptist, a monthly magazine issued by the Baptist Church by the Hon. Pastor C. Haddon Parry*. The copies which have survived, despite some missing months, are for the years 1936-1941 and cover the period leading up to the outbreak of the Second World War.

Secondary Sources:

Ayres, James	*The Shell Book of the Home in Britain* (Faber, 1981)
Beresford, Maurice	*History on the Ground* (Methuen, 1971)
Betjeman, Sir John	*In Praise of churches* (John Murray, 1996)
Brunskill, R.W.	*Illustrated Handbook of Vernacular Architecture* (Faber, 1978)
	Houses and Cottages of Britain (Gollancz, 1997)
	Timber Building in Britain (Gollancz, 1985)
Burke, Gerald	*Towns in the Making* (Edward Arnold, 1979)
Coward, Mary, et al,	*Rickford: A History of a North Somerset Village* (Rickford History Society, 2000)
Dunning, Robert	*Christianity in Somerset* (Somerset County Council, 1976)
Edwards, David L.	*Christian England Its Story to the Reformation* (Collins, 1981)
Hey, David	*The Oxford Companion to Local and Family History* (OUP, 1996)
Hibbs, John,	*The Country Chapel* (David and Charles, 1988)
Jones, Anthea	*A Thousand Years of the English Parish* (Windrush Press, 2001)
Leech, Joseph	*The Church Goer: Rural Rides or Calls at Country Churches, Second Series* (Bristol: John Ridler, 1850)
Moon, Norman	*Education for Ministry, Bristol Baptist College 1679 -1979* (Bristol Baptist College, 1979)
Muir, Richard	*Reading the Landscape* (Book Club Associates, 1981)
Penoyre, Jane	*The Traditional Houses of Somerset* (Somerset County Council, 2005)
Quiney, Anthony	*House and Home: A History of the Small English House* (BBC Publications, 1986)
Reid, Richard	*The Shell Book of Cottages* (Michael Joseph, 1977)
Shorney, David	*Protestant Nonconformity and Roman Catholicism* (PRO, 1996)
Taylor, Christopher	*Village and Farmstead* (George Philip & Sons, 1983)
Taylor, Tim	*The Time Team What happened When* (Channel 4 Books, 2006)
The publications of	*The Somerset Vernacular Building Research Group*
	The Vernacular Architecture Group
Watts, Michael R.	*The Chapel and the Nation: Non-Conformity and the Local Historian* (Historical Association, 1996)
Yorke, Trevor,	*Tracing the History of Villages* (Countryside Books, 2001)
	The Holy Bible Authorised (King James) version (OUP, nd)
	The New English Bible – New Testament (Oxford UP and Cambridge UP, 1961)

[1] David Hey, *The Oxford Companion to Local and Family History*, p.34.

[2] ibid p.34.

[3] Norman S. Moon, *Education for Ministry Bristol Baptist College 1679–1979,* p.1.

[4] *150 years of the Baptist Itinerant Society*, Bristol Record Office, ref. 40798/cc/11d.

[5] Protestant Dissenters Certificate December 30th 1776, copy in BLHS archives.

[6] Dissenters Certificate for a Chapel dated 19th November 1808, ditto.

[7] Dissenters Certificate for the Methodists dated 6th August 1805, ditto.

[8] *The Oxford Companion to Local and Family History* (1996), p. 310.

[9] Richard Muir, *Reading the Landscape* (1981), pp.153–179.
Maurice Beresford, *History on the Ground*, and C. Taylor, *Village and Farmstead* .

[10] The Holy Bible (King James version) St. Matthew, ch.18, v.20

[11] Dissenters Records, copies in BLHS archive.

[12] ibid

[13] ibid

[14] Baptist Church Record – Blagdon Church Book (Volume 1), p.3.

[15] Dissenters Records, BLHS archive – A note by Kathleen Rose Jones (n. d.)

[16] Blagdon Church Book (Vol. 1) pp. 3 -4.

[17] ibid p.2. from pasted in printed extracts from the Bristol Baptists Itinerant Society.

[18] ibid p.4.

[19] ibid p.4.

[20] ibid p.5.

[21] ibid p.5.

[22] ibid p.6.

[23] ibid pp. 6 -7.

[24] ibid p.8.

[25] ibid p.7.

[26] ibid p.7.

[27] ibid pp.11-12 printed and pasted-in extracts.

[28] Mary Coward, *Rickford, A History of a North Somerset Village* pp. 9–10.

[29] ibid p.12.

[30] ibid p.27.

[31] ibid p.22–23.

[32] ibid p.23.

[33] Joseph Leech, *The Church Goer: Rural Rides or Calls at Country Churches*, Second Series pp.66-68.

[34] *Oxford Companion to Local and Family History*, pp.325.

[35] The Time Team, *What Happened When*, Tim Taylor, p.291.

[36] ibid p.282.

[37] The New English Bible – New Testament, Matthew ch.28, v.20

The Forest of Mendip Lodge
Province of Somerset
1962–1999

Ray Grimstead

Introduction

Blagdon Local History Society is grateful to Ray Grimstead and his fellow Freemasons for recording this brief history of their Lodge. The history outlines how the Lodge started, how premises were found, and the initiatives and leadership that led eventually to the establishment of the Forest of Mendip Lodge.

This article follows *The Baptist Church in Blagdon* because the two fellowships were linked by circumstance and coincidence, as one came to an end and the other made a new beginning, in a building that provided suitable accommodation for both organisations. Apart from these few editorial words of introduction, Ray Grimstead is the author of the history of The Forest of Mendip Lodge.

How it started

The Forest of Mendip Lodge (No. 8019) was formed in 1965 and its successful creation was largely the work of W. Bro. Reg Young with the support of fourteen other Brethren who with him became Founder Members.

Reg Young was the musical director of the Blagdon Carol Party, which used to tour the village and surrounding countryside before Christmas, dressed in Dickensian costume. In February 1962, at their annual dinner at the Star Hotel in Wells, Reg was approached by several male members of the Carol Party who suggested that it would be a good idea to form a Masonic Lodge in Blagdon. He asked why, if it was such a good idea, they did not do something about it! They explained that they were young and inexperienced Masons and thought it would be more appropriate for him to get things started.

Fig. 1 - Rickford Hall
(Neil Bentham August 2007)

Suitable Premises

Reg decided that the embryo Lodge would need to find a regular meeting place. It happened that three months later he was having his hair trimmed by Mr R.C. Sampson (later Bro. Sampson) a local oracle, and inquired whether the Baptists were still using the hall at Rickford. He was delighted to learn that they had vacated their premises a month earlier. Reg telephoned Sir John Wills the same day and an appointment was made for the following day. Sir John was willing for the proposed Lodge to have the use of the hall and very relieved that the premises were likely to be occupied.

Having secured the premises, W. Bro. Reg Young's next move was to visit the Provincial Grand Master for Somerset, the R.W. Bro. Brigadier Cazenove. At first the Provincial Grand Master seemed very doubtful whether there was sufficient terrain to draw on, but he was reminded that there were no Lodges at all in the Chew Valley nor any between Nailsea and Keynsham. Eventually he gave the project his blessing. W. Bro. Young then proceeded to lobby his Masonic friends and fifteen Masons were pleased to become Founders.

The records show that twelve meetings were held and that there were many changes to the personnel. Some of the most eager opted out when an estimated figure of £2,300 was mooted as being the realistic cost in total for starting and equipping the new Lodge in the early 1960s.

On 21st March 1963 the Founders unanimously agreed to proceed with the formation of the Lodge, and on 19th September 1963 this was confirmed and W. Bro. Young was nominated as Master Elect. Meanwhile the Founders, in negotiation with Sir John Wills, proposed that they should carry out the necessary repairs to the building. This did not meet with his wishes. Instead he generously offered £500 towards the repairs to be repaid as rental over ten years. The Lodge has continued to pay for the upkeep and repair of the building and in return they have paid a modest annual rent.

The Name

The Founders had unanimously agreed that the title of the Lodge should be 'Rock of Ages', which they thought to be appropriate since the premises would be only a few hundred yards from the well known landmark. However, the Provincial Grand Master would not give his approval. He argued that this could have only a Christian connotation and as the Constitution accepted all creeds who believed in an Almighty Being the name was not acceptable. He suggested the Lodge should be called 'Forest of Mendip', a name which found favour with all the Founders.

The Consecration

The next task was to find a Lodge to sponsor the petition, and as W. Bro. Young was well known to the members of Birnbeck Lodge at Weston-super-Mare, where he had been organist for a number of years, they readily agreed to act as sponsors. On 15th December 1964 the Founders attended a regular meeting of Birnbeck Lodge when the Petition was duly endorsed. In March 1965 the furniture and regalia was delivered and five rehearsals were held in preparation for the Consecration.

This ceremony was held at 4 o'clock on Tuesday 25th May 1965 and was carried out by the then Provincial Grand Master, the R.W. Bro. Brigadier A. De Lerisson Cazenove, assisted by the Deputy Provincial Grand Master, V.W. Bro. Henry Frampton and members of Provincial Grand Lodge. In replying to the Master's toast on that occasion W. Bro. Reg Young expressed his thanks to all his fellow Founders and paid particular tribute to the encouragement and very active assistance he had received from the Treasurer, W. Bro. Percy Moore.

Forest of Mendip Lodge has a great deal for which to thank W. Bro. Reg. Young: not only was he a Founder and the first Worshipful Master, he also served as Organist from 1966 until the year prior to his death in 1984 in his 101st year. It is fitting that his portrait hangs in the Lodge in recognition of this service.

The Spiral Staircase

Attendance at the early meetings of the Lodge stretched the accommodation to its limit because of the large number of visiting Brethren. One frequent visitor was Bro. Bill Whalley who, early in 1965, was approached and it was suggested to him that in his professional capacity he would be aware when demolitions were being carried out in Bristol. The reason for the approach was that the Lodge hoped to increase its accommodation by installing a spiral staircase to the balcony (fig. 2). A few months later he informed the Lodge that it would give him much pleasure to present it to the Lodge. It was fitted the following September under the guidance of W. Bro. Norman Minto – it fitted perfectly and incidentally consists of 15 steps.

The Banner

On Friday 24th April 1981 the Presentation and dedication of the Lodge Banner took place, the ceremony being performed by V.W. Bro. Herbert E. Dyke, the deputy Provincial Grand Master. The banner was very kindly presented by Bro. Fred Rainey.

Fig. 2 - Interior of Rickford Hall
(Neil Bentham March 2001)

Silver Jubilee

On 25th May 1990 the Lodge celebrated its Silver Jubilee and the meeting was attended by the Provincial Grand Master, the R.W. Bro. Stanley H.A.F. Hopkins, together with 19 Past Masters, 16 Members and 39 other visitors. Over the years the Lodge has regularly attracted many visiting brethren, no doubt largely due to its attractive and unique premises.

The Festive Board

When the Lodge was first formed, after each meeting it was customary to adjourn to the upper floor of the Seymour Arms for the 'Festive Board', then for a number of years these meals were provided in Burrington Village Hall. In more recent years Brethren have gathered for their meal in the Blagdon Village Club.

Charity

As with all Lodges within the United Grand Lodge of England, the Forest of Mendip Lodge donates a prescribed annual sum on behalf of each member to The Grand Charity of Freemasons. As well as supporting Masonic charities, the Grand Charity gives donations to many non-Masonic charities such as disaster funds (for example, £100,000 was given to the Kosova Appeal), and in 1998 it donated a total of £503,000 to 173 hospices in England and Wales. This brought the total amount of grants to hospices since 1984 to £2,432,850. The Grand Charity also makes grants, very often in an enabling role, principally to organisations and other charities in support of youth, general welfare and medical research (for example, the Alzheimers Research Trust has received the first instalment of a £125,000 grant).

In addition to making their contribution to the Grand Charity (£462 in the two years 1997/98), the Forest of Mendip Lodge aims to donate to local worthy causes from time to time. In the two years 1997/98: £500 was donated to the Blagdon Mini-bus Appeal; £200 towards the Blagdon Playground equipment; and £58, plus a large teddy bear, to the Children's Hospice South West.

Membership

Since its consecration in 1965, 65 men have been initiated into Freemasonry in the Forest of Mendip Lodge and 64 brethren have joined from other Lodges. At 31st December 1998 the Lodge membership numbered 54 and, contrary to original predictions, members are drawn from a wide area. Although almost half come from the Chew Valley, others come regularly from such places as Weston-super-Mare, Bridgwater, Bristol, Portishead, Clutton and the Forest of Dean. A few have moved to other parts of the country too far away to attend meetings but still keep in touch.

The wide variety of occupations from which they come provides for a great breadth of experience. The Lodge has welcomed as members newsagents, farmers, sales executives, builders, local authority officers, hauliers, solicitors, a vicar, police officers, heating engineers, motor mechanics, civil servants, a postmaster, electrical engineers, a sawyer and a carpenter, to name but a few!

Open Days

On 4th June 1995, conforming to the principle of more openness about Freemasons' activities, the Lodge held its first Open Day. Members of the public were invited to visit the Masonic Hall at Rickford and given the opportunity to ask questions about Freemasonry. The event proved to be a considerable success and we are now planning to repeat the event in July 1999.

Bro. Secretary W. Bro. R. E. Grimstead (30th May 1999)

Footnote from the author, September 2007

The Forest of Mendip Lodge has made steady progress in the eight years since the above history was written. The July 1999 Open Day was very successful, and we were pleased to greet many members of the public. The Deputy Provincial Grand Master V. W. Vernon Harding welcomed our visitors and delivered a short address describing Freemasonry. This was followed by a question and answer session and a short film about the United Grand Lodge of England. The Lodge continues to donate to national and local charities; as a notable example of the latter, the Lodge raised sufficient funds to provide three Electric High Dependency Beds for the Transplant unit of Southmead Hospital. Fourteen new members have been initiated in the Lodge since September 1999, and eight brethren have joined from other lodges. The current membership stands at 52 and in 2008 we will celebrate our 300th meeting.
Ray Grimstead (Bro. secretary 1996 – 2001)

Sources

An account of the origins of the formation of this Lodge, by W. Bro. R. T. Young The Origin and Short History of the Forest of Mendip Lodge No. 8019, delivered on the occasion of the Lodge's Silver Jubilee, 25th May 1990, by Bro. P.J.W. Webster The Grand Charity Annual Report, 30th November 1998.
The Compass Magazine.
Lodge Minute and Record Books.

The Methodist Church in Blagdon

Neil Bentham

The history of the Methodists in Blagdon begins with John Wesley (1703-1791) and his brother Charles Wesley (1707-1788), who began the Methodist movement in 1738. Two years later, in 1740, the Methodist Society was founded.

Fig. 1 – John Wesley (1703-1791)
(author's photograph of a print in Blagdon Methodist chapel)

*'The term 'Methodist' originated in the University of Oxford, when certain students,
including John and Charles Wesley, formed themselves into what was also called,
'The Holy Club,' and because they lived by 'Method', the name was given to them.
It was, essentially, a nickname, but over time it gradually became the name by which
John Wesley's societies were known and developed into the Methodist Church we now know.
In its widest sense it covers not only the work of John Wesley and his followers, but also
of George Whitefield and Howell Harris, represented today by the Presbyterian Church
of Wales, known at one time as Calvanistic Methodism and includes the societies formed
by the Countess of Huntingdon. These apart, Methodism as derived from Wesley, was
one and undivided during his lifetime, but following his death in 1791 there were several
secessions, all of which maintained the name Methodist, but which are distinguished by
other titles and of course other features and emphasis...*

*Fig. 2 – Statue of Charles Wesley
(1707-1788)*

*Situated in the grounds of the
New Room, the Horsefair, Bristol.*

(author's photograph)

*'The first secession was in 1797 when under the leadership of Alexander Kilham, a
Wesleyan Minister, the* **Methodist New Connexion** *was formed. In the first half of the
nineteenth century further breakaways led to the formation of other bodies. Such were* **the
Primitive Methodists** *in 1807 led by Hugh Bourne and William Clowes. In 1815 a*

group known as **The Bible Christians** *(the only group not to include the word Methodist in their title) was formed in the West Country, but they were an off-shoot of the parent body. A small group to be known as* **Protestant Methodists** *was formed in Leeds in 1827 and a further group known as the* **Wesleyan Methodist Association** *was formed in 1836…in 1849 certain men determined to reform Wesleyan Methodism… became known as Wesleyan Reformers…they eventually joined forces with the Protestant Methodists and the Wesleyan Methodist Association to constitute what became known as the* **United Methodist Free Churches** *(1857). Not all the reformers joined this united church, but formed their own under the title* **Wesleyan Reform Union** *…fifty years on, three of the divided groups came together – the United Methodist Free Churches, the Methodist New Connection and the Bible Christians to form the* **United Methodist Church** *(1907). In 1932 the final union was consummated by the coming together of the United Methodist Church, the Primitive Methodist Church and the Wesleyan Methodist Church… Thus today we think of the Methodist Church as one and for practical purposes… it is one…*

'One further aspect… ought to be noted. In 1806 there were secessions from the main body which became known as **Independent Methodist Churches** *many of which continue to this day…also, there is the Salvation Army, not an off shoot of Methodism…but the founder of the Salvation Army, William Booth (1829-1912) was, in his early years, a Methodist Minister first in the Wesleyan Reform movement and later in the Methodist New Connexion'.*[1]

Mention was made earlier of the Countess of Huntingdon (and her Connexion). *'Selina Hastings was the Countess of Huntingdon (1707-1791) who financed the Calvinist branch of the Methodist movement led by George Whitefield whom she appointed her chaplain in 1751. She built chapels in London and at fashionable Bath, Brighton, and Tunbridge Wells, and in 1767 founded a theological college in Breconshire. Services were conducted in conformity with the Church of England, even after the Methodist break with the Anglican Church in 1779. At the time of the ecclesiastical census of 1851 the Connexion had over one hundred chapels'.*[2] Pevsner describes the chapel in Bath as, *'built in 1765, the exceedingly pretty little villa facade is that of the Countess's own house'.*[3] The chapel now contains the permanent exhibition of *'the Building of Bath Museum'.*

Although inspired by Wesley, the organisation of the Methodist Church was established by others. Wesley did, however, instigate the first Annual Conference in 1744, and this in time led to the establishment of a four tier system. Geographical districts were set up that held twice-yearly Synods. Local Circuits were selected, usually consisting of ten or more Churches, which held quarterly meetings. Of these four meetings two were special, one being devoted to the support of lay or local preachers and the other for the general administration of the circuit. Finally each local church or chapel was, and still is, administered by a selected group of officers who are responsible for both the fabric of the building and the spiritual welfare of its members.[4] This system has worked for over 260 years. In contrast to the Church of England, each Methodist minister is invited to serve a church or, in these days, perhaps more than one church, for four or five years duration. One minister may, by invitation, be appointed as a Superintendent minister, and another, or an eminent layman, elected as Chairman of a District, so in effect there is a rotation system that enables each minister to take up a fresh 'challenge' and, equally, prevents their flock becoming moribund by the repetition of similar preaching themes.

Wesley built his first headquarters in 1739, the oldest Methodist building in the world, the New Room, known locally as John Wesley's Chapel, in the Horsefair in Bristol. It was, *'enlarged in 1748'.*[5] From there he began to travel the length and breadth of the country, *'preaching the glad tidings of salvation'*, and *'endeavouring to do good'.*[6]

At the outset of his career Wesley was ordained as a priest in the Church of England, and, although he developed the practice of open air preaching that attracted many large crowds to hear his message of salvation, hope and comfort to the ordinary people, his church services were initially held in the local parish churches. Wesley preached at many of the village churches near to Blagdon and that would have drawn interested villagers to walk, or travel by horse and cart, to hear his message.

Research into the Methodist Church records held in John Wesley's Chapel at the Horsefair, Bristol (fig. 4), and the Library at Wesley College Bristol, indicate that there is no record of the Wesleys having preached in Blagdon, but John Wesley's preaching in the nearby villages is well documented.

From the journals John Wesley kept one gets a sense of the vital energy the man sustained over his long life. He preached 40,000 sermons and travelled 250,000 miles on horseback to meetings far and wide to teach, debate and expound the love of God. He had a driven desire to defeat evil and ungodliness wherever he found it and bring to those, both poor and without hope, the message from the Gospels that they were just as needed and just as much valued as others who seemed to have everything that the world considered to be riches.

Fig. 3 – Statue of John Wesley
Outside John Wesley's chapel, the Horsefair, Bristol
(author's photograph)

Fig. 4 – Interior of the New Room, known locally as John Wesley's Chapel
(author's photograph)

At the outset of Wesley's ministry his style was to take the Word of God to the people and the following examples are taken from his journals. Although some are much further afield others are local to Blagdon, but they all convey something of the way in which his itinerant style of ministry was to inspire supporters from Lands End to Scotland, and eventually, in membership numbers, become third in size only to the Church of England and the Catholic Church.

However, not all clerical colleagues welcomed him, and Wesley's journal entry for Monday 23rd April 1739 reads,

'On a repeated invitation, I went to Pensford, about five miles from Bristol. I sent to the Minister, to ask leave to preach in the church; but having waited some time and received no answer, I called on many of the people who were gathered together in an open place.'[7]

'Monday 10 February 1746 – I preached at Paulton; on Thursday noon at Shepton Mallet; and at Oak Hill in the evening. The next morning I walked (It being scarce possible to ride, because of the frost) to Coleford'[8]

On his visit to Clutton on Friday 26th September 1757, he says, 'I preached, at nine, to a small congregation of earnest people at Clutton[9]

Saturday 26th August 1780, We had our Quarterly Meeting at Redruth, where all was love and harmony.
Sunday 27th. It was supposed, twenty thousand people were assembled at the amphitheatre in Gwennap. And yet all, I was informed, could hear distinctly, in the fair, calm evening.
Monday 28th . I preached at Wadebridge and Port Isaac;
Tuesday 29th, at Camelford and Launceston. Hence we hastened toward Bristol, by way of Wells; where (the weather being intensely hot, so that we could not well bear the Room) I preached on the shady side of the market-place, on, 'By grace are ye saved, through faith'.[10]

Another entry, on Thursday 14th October 1780, states, 'I read prayers and preached in Clutton Church; But it was with great difficulty, because of my hoarseness; which so increased, that in four and twenty hours I could scarce speak at all. At night I used my never failing remedy, bruised garlic applied to the soles of the feet. This cured my hoarseness in six hours; In one hour it cured my lumbago, the pain in the small of my back, which I had had ever since I came from Cornwall.' [11]

In his Journal (no. 20) that covers the three and a half years from September 4th 1782 until June 28th 1786 he writes, 'Wednesday, September 4, 1782.- I preached in the market-house at Tiverton; Thursday, 5, at Halburton, Taunton, and South Brent. Friday, 6. about ten I preached at Shipham, a little town on the side of the Mendiff [sic] almost wholly inhabited by miners who dig up lapis calaminaris. I was surprised to see such a congregation at so short a warning; and their deep and serious attention seemed to presage, that some of them will profit by what they hear. In the afternoon we went on to Bristol'. [12]

'After preaching at Roade, Pensford, Trowbridge and Freshford, on Friday, 13, I preached at Bath.
Sunday, 15 (September 1782) I had a far greater number of communicants than usual…
On Monday and Tuesday I preached at Chew-Magna, at Sutton, Stoke, and Clutton: In my way thither, I saw a famous monument of antiquity, at Stanton Drew; supposed to have remained there between two and three thousand years. It was undoubtedly a Druid's temple, consisting of a smaller and a larger circle of huge stones set on end, one would think by some power more than human. Indeed such stones have been used for divine worship, nearly, if not quite, from the time of the flood.' On the following days I preached at many other little places'.[13]

His journal records a visit to Churchill on Saturday 11th March 1786, 'I rode over to Churchill, about 12 miles from Bristol, where Dr. Barry read prayers and I preached to a serious congregation.'[14]

We do not know which Blagdon villagers went to hear John Wesley preach or where they watched and listened while he conducted divine service or addressed gatherings of the idly curious, or the simply questioning, or even the cynic or doubter, but we do know that in the almost twenty years after he preached at St John the Baptist parish church, Churchill, a small group of believers had been so inspired by the preaching that Wesley and his disciples delivered that they took the first steps to establish a Methodist presence in Blagdon.

The earliest Dissenters record that we have in the Society's archive is dated August 6th 1805 (fig. 5), and in copperplate handwriting it states:

To the Right Rev. Father in God, Richard, Lord Bishop of Bath and Wells, or his Register We whose names are underwritten hereby certify to your Lordship, that a house in the occupation of John and Hannah Bond, in the Village and Parish of Blagdon, in the County of Somerset, is intended to be occasionally used for the religious Worship of Almighty God, by a Congregation of Protestant Dissenters, commonly called Methodists; and request that the same may be registered in your Lordship's Registry, pursuant to the Act in that case made and provided, and a Certificate of the same given accordingly.

Blagdon
Aug. 6th 1805.

The Mark of 'X' Hannah Bond
William Warley
William Gallop
Edward Gallop
John Haines
John Filer
Joseph White

Certificate granted hereon
August 10th. 1805.

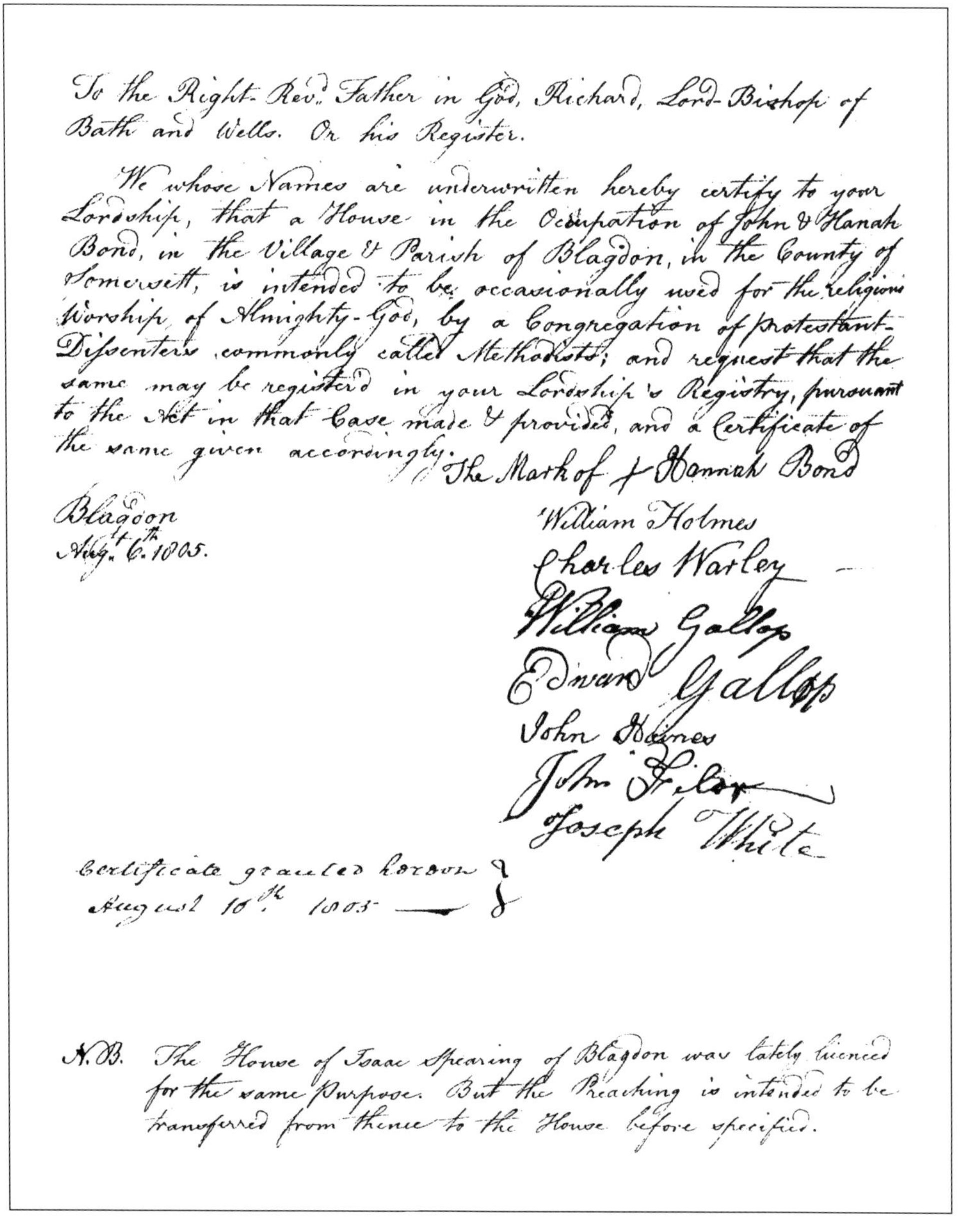

Fig. 5 – Dissenter's certificate August 1805

Written vertically down the left hand side of the request is: 'The House of Isaac Spearing of Blagdon was lately licenced for the same purpose. But the Preaching is intended to be transferred from thence to the House before specified'.[15]

Since the address is not given, we are uncertain which house belonged to John and Hannah Bond. So it is conjecture that the house we know as Chapel Grove Court (fig. 7), on the south side of the Bath Road alongside the narrow footpath that leads up towards Rhodyate, was the Bond family home. It is also assumed that the cottage had a large garden, perched high up above the level of the original turnpike. Also, following the foundation of the Primitive Methodist secession in 1807 mentioned earlier, this coincides with the building of a permanent Methodist chapel on the site of the original cottage garden (fig. 6).

The archives of the Methodist Church in North Somerset, kept by Mrs Jean Darby of Congresbury, give a date of 1807 for the building of the chapel at a cost of £400. The building was to serve the Methodist cause for the next hundred years, and the above record also shows that, in 1891, renovations were carried out at a cost of £110.

It is a striking coincidence that two Bristol business men, neither of whom was born in Blagdon and each of whom made their fortunes in totally different enterprises, would within a year or so of each other both finance and build two out of the three new churches in Blagdon in the early years of the twentieth century. These two business men were Mr W.H. Wills (1830-1911) of Coombe Lodge, with his tobacco industry, and Mr Simon Sidney Hill (1829-1908) of Langford House, with his shipping empire.

The history of St Andrew's parish church, and the rebuilding of the nave and restoration of the 15th century tower by William Henry Wills (later Lord Winterstoke) is the subject of a separate article, but this article continues with the equally philanthropic generosity of Mr Hill to the cause of Methodism.

Simon Sidney Hill was, by any measure, a most prolific and generous benefactor to the Methodists of this area. He was born in Bristol in 1829 and little is known about his early life, except that as a young man he used to visit a Mr William Bobbett in Bristol, whose niece, Mary Ann Bobbett, kept house for him. This young lady was educated at the Friend's Boarding School at Sidcot, and at York. She attracted the attention of Mr Hill and seven years later she became his wife.

Hill suffered a setback in health that caused him to give up his drapery business in 1857, and he was advised to take a sea voyage. He set out for New Zealand, but when his ship berthed at Cape Town he decided to stay in South Africa.

Fig. 6 – Wesleyan Chapel, Bath Road, Blagdon - founded in 1807
(BLHS Archives)

Fig. 7– Chapel Grove Court (August 2007)
(author's photograph)

Eventually he entered into partnership with a Mr William Savage and the firm of Savage and Hill, Colonial and General Merchants, began trading from Port Elizabeth. The business prospered and in 1864 Hill returned to London both healthy and wealthy to direct his firm's large shipping interests, and in that same year he married Mary Bobbett. She had moved from Bristol to Wrington to a house known as Sidney Villa, close to Barley Wood, the former home of Hannah More (1745-1833).

In 1865 the couple set out for South Africa, but nine years later Mrs Hill's health failed and they returned to England on 8th April 1874. They decided to live in Bournemouth because of its mild climate, but after only five weeks' residence there Mary Hill died on 7th December 1874. In an attempt to cope with his grief, Hill returned to South Africa, but he could not settle and returned to England in 1877. He then bought Langford House Estate (fig. 8), settled down and devoted himself to good works (fig. 9).

Fig. 8 – Langford House August 2007
(author's photograph)

His readiness to help the poor, aid the sick, and provide for widows and orphans became almost legendary. The poor received weekly gifts of shoes, clothing and food, and at Christmas the contents of each parcel were noted so that the same things were not included in the next Christmas parcels. His benefactions were quietly and unostentatiously performed, but his public generosity could not pass unnoticed.

As a result of Simon Sidney Hill's business success and his conversion at a Methodist meeting in Bristol sixteen years later in 1907, he generously offered to provide the Methodists of Blagdon with a new church at Street End. It was necessary to sell the old chapel to help fund the new building. Thus, the old chapel, complete with a stable at the rear for the visiting preacher's horse, languished unused and empty other than for domestic storage for the next 60 years, until the whole site was again sold in the late 1960s. The detached chapel building was subsequently converted into domestic accommodation, as an extension to the existing cottage. The buildings were linked by a tiny entrance hall which bridged the small gap between the two parts.

The present owners of Chapel Grove Court, Mr & Mrs Alan Barwick, inform us that there is a wedding dress nailed to the roof of the old chapel – but whose dress, and why it was nailed to the roof, is a mystery as yet unsolved.

Although there is a hundred year gap after the above dissenters' request to the Bishop, the Barwicks have kindly made available to the Society a copy of an indenture dated 1907 that records some of the owners:

'Indenture made the Seventh day of November one thousand nine hundred and seven (7th November 1907), between Theophilus Harding of Blagdon in the County of Somerset, Farmer George Parker Caple of Stanton Prior in the same County, Farmer Henry Sheppard of Ubley in the same County, Farmer Thomas Caple of West Harptree in the same County, Farmer George Gallop of Williton in the same County, Shopkeeper (herein after called the Vendors) of the one part and Samuel Filer of Blagdon aforesaid Carpenter (herein after called the Purchaser) of the other part. Whereas by an indenture dated the ninth day of January one thousand eight hundred and seventy eight (9th January 1878) and made between William Gallop and William Hellier of the first part the Reverend Joseph Cade (Superintendent Minister in the Circuit of the Wesleyan Methodist Connection in which the heriditaments therein after and hereinafter described were situate)...'

(A copy of the complete indenture is kept in the BLHS archive in Court Lodge.)[16]

Fig. 9 – Simon Sidney Hill
(Methodist Archives, Jean Darby)

In 1906, the new Methodist chapel at Street End in Blagdon was built in memory of Hill's close friend, Mr T.F.C. May. They were converted together at the same meeting in Bristol. This event is recorded in a large foundation stone built into the east wall of the church beneath the east window. The incised inscription reads:

THIS STONE WAS LAID
TO THE GLORY OF GOD, AND IN MEMORY OF
THOMAS FRANCIS CHRISTOPHER MAY, OF COTHAM BRISTOL
ON WEDNESDAY OCTOBER 17TH 1906
BY HIS WIDOW

Sidney Hill's generosity is commemorated in a marble plaque inside the chapel porch as shown in fig. 10.

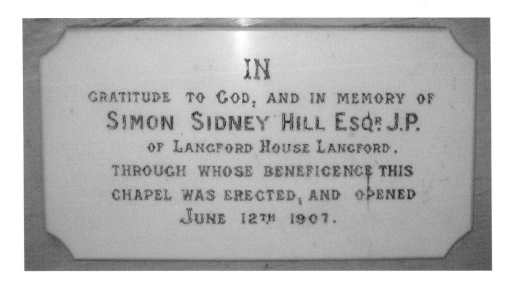

Fig. 10 – Plaque in memory of Simon Sidney Hill
(author's photograph)

Other foundation stones may be seen, low down on the north wall of the chapel near the entrance porch, but these do not always record the names of those founding Methodists. Those that are named are, 'Laid by Mrs Dyer,' 'Laid by Arthur Loveless,' 'In Memory of G. and M. Harding,' 'This stone was laid by E. Kelly.' Those recorded by initials are, 'Laid by W.G.G. on behalf of the Sunday School,' 'In Memory of W.G.,' 'This stone was laid In Memory of A.G., and E.T.', 'Laid by H.S. on behalf of the Class.'

An entry in the Blagdon school log dated 17th October 1906 records that the children were given a day's holiday for '*laying stones at the new Wesleyan Chapel*'.

The new chapel had two tall spirelets, one at each side of the central east window. Approximately fifty years after the spirelets were first built they presumably became unsafe, and were removed. The photograph below (fig 11) shows the church as Sidney Hill had it built, and, one hundred years later, fig.12 shows the church as it is today.

Sidney Hill's building boom also created other buildings in the villages within a few miles of his eventual home at Langford House. Listed below, in chronological order, are the memorial churches he had built:

1881 – Churchill Methodist Memorial Church, built in memory of his wife who had died on 7th December 1874, a few years before he bought Langford House. Mrs Mary Ann Hill was originally buried at Arnos Vale Cemetery in Bristol. On completion of the church, and its dedication on 10th March 1881, her remains were removed to a mausoleum at the south side of the church, and for the rest of his life Hill placed a rose on the grave of his wife before the service each Sunday morning. Originally the church did not have an entrance porch but Hill added one in 1898. He also built a hall or schoolroom adjacent to the church where he could hold secular meetings, and appointed Endowment Trustees, who were different trustees to that of the church, to administer it.

1893 – Shipham Memorial Methodist Church, erected to the memory of William Bobbett, his wife's uncle, the class leader who brought Sidney Hill to a realization of Christ.

1897 – Cheddar Methodist Memorial Church, replaced the first Wesleyan Methodist chapel that was built in 1800. This building served until 1853 when it was judged to be too small, and a new chapel was built. Before the end of the century this building had also become inadequate for the growing Society, and an approach was made to Hill. Once again his generosity and love of Methodism was demonstrated and he willingly agreed to both fund and furnish the new church we see today. Hill also had the Cheddar manse built at the same time. The house, after 93 years of use by a succession of Methodist ministers, was sold in 1990. He also built and furnished the manse at Banwell.

Fig. 11 - Blagdon Methodist Chapel as built in 1907.
(David Lock collection)

Fig. 12- Blagdon Methodist Chapel August 2007
(author's photograph)

1900 – Sandford Methodist Church was built at a cost of £1700 and was called the Centenary Chapel. The original chapel was turned into the schoolroom.

1906 – Blagdon Memorial Methodist Church built with attached schoolroom and detached house.

Simon Sidney Hill also contributed generously to the Anglican parish church of St John the Baptist at Churchill. He also furthered the Wesleyan Methodist cause during his stay at Port Elizabeth in South Africa, holding the church offices of Sunday School Superintendent, class leader, chapel and circuit steward. In addition, Hill was a generous contributor to the building of the Wesleyan chapel at Lympsham, and to improvements at the Wesleyan Chapels at Wedmore, Axbridge and Wrington. He was made a justice of the peace of Somerset in 1886 and served on the Bench, always tempering justice with mercy.

In addition to the five Methodist chapels, he also funded the building in 1897 of the Churchill clocktower and drinking fountain at the junction of Front Street and Back Street (now known as Dinghurst Road). The clocktower was built to commemorate the Diamond Jubilee of Queen Victoria. At the same time, an oak tree, with a semi-circular matching iron railing surround and a small area of ornamental grounds, was planted near The Nelson Inn.

Sidney Hill's teetotal zeal was revealed when, in order to build these features, he demolished some small cottages that he felt were so near to the Nelson Inn that their proximity would prove too great a temptation for the inhabitants to drink away their earnings. However, he built the Cottage Homes nearby and paid the displaced residents a weekly sum to live there.

The Churchill Cottage Homes (fig. 13) and the Victoria Jubilee Langford Homes (fig. 14) were two of Sidney Hill's most ambitious projects and represent the last of the many charitable foundations that he created and endowed.

At the Churchill Homes (fig. 13), the plaque in the archway forming the principal entrance to the quadrangle around which the twelve dwellings are set reads:

Sidney Hill Churchill, Wesleyan Cottage Homes.

*These Homes together with the Matron's House were
erected on Freehold land in the year of Our Lord
1907 by Sidney Hill, Esq., J.P., of Langford House
in the Parish of Churchill, to the Glory of God and
for the accommodation of aged persons being members
of, or adherents to the Wesleyan Methodist Society, who
have lived for the last three years within a radius of
three miles from this spot.*

*Fig. 13 – Wesleyan Cottage homes, Churchill
(author's photograph)*

To provide the site for the homes, land was purchased known as 'Vicarage Close'.
This extended to just over five and a half acres, of which about one and a half acres
was set aside for the buildings and gardens. The remaining four acres, to the south of
the site, were described in the Trust Deed as, 'never to be built upon but used for
grazing purposes only and may be let for the purpose of rent.'

The outward appearance was Sidney Hill's own conception inspired by the picture 'Harbour of Refuge' by Frederick Walker, painted in 1872 and now in the Tate Gallery in London. The homes were built by Messrs Ford and Son of Cheddar at a cost of nearly £15,000. The clerk of works was Mr Bowden and the architects were Messrs T.B. Silcock, B.Sc., R.S.I., and S.S. Reay, F.R.I.B.A., of Bath and London. The architects' drawing of the scheme was hung in the Royal Academy Exhibition in 1906.

The Victoria Jubilee Langford Homes

In 1888 and 1889 Sidney Hill bought and cleared a site that in 1812 contained an orchard, a house and six cottages, together with a tanyard, that bordered the turnpike road that led from Bristol to Exeter and ran, at that time, through the middle of Langford. This land was to be the future site for his Jubilee Homes. He also purchased Rookery Farm, Congresbury, with its 65 acres and another 22 acres of land known as Smallway. These two parcels of land were to be an endowment for the provision of income to maintain the future homes. The total cost was £14,300 plus a further £1,300 to re-instate Rookery Farm. From the endowment, rental totalling £229 per annum was secured. In addition to the maintenance of the properties this sum was to provide £30 per annum for each of the tenants of the homes.

The imposing Jubilee Homes containing six dwellings was completed in 1890 and commissioned and endowed in 1891 and was built to a high standard. Externally the homes are built of local stone in a late Victorian style of architecture. The two storey building, under a main, steeply pitched gabled roof, with subservient smaller pitched dormer roofs at right angles, form a strong rhythm. Tall bold chimney stacks are symmetrically disposed at ridge and eaves. The south front elevation, with projecting wings at each end with vertical semi-circular bay windows, has a symmetrical façade with a central projecting full height bay emphasising the main entrance. To either side at ground floor level are flanking bay windows under a continuous eyebrow mono pitched roof all in matching plain red tiles with the main roof. A carved cartouche of the Hill crest fills the higher central gable.

The Homes are set within their own spacious grounds that are surrounded by a low wall on the street frontage, surmounted by ornate cast-iron railings. A semi-circular gravel drive with gateways at either end provides access and egress, with planted beds and box hedges, again repeating the symmetrical layout in the horizontal plane. A mature redwood tree at the east end dominates the south facing elevation.

Fig. 14 – The Victoria Jubilee Langford Homes
(author's photograph)

Langford House Estate was to be Simon Sidney Hill's home for the last thirty one years of his life and he settled there as a gentleman farmer and public benefactor. He developed Langford House in a flamboyant Victorian style and even built luxurious quarters for his famous Red Scots Shorthorns. 'Bullock Palaces' they were nicknamed, and with their dormer windows and separate compartments for each beast they were something unheard of at the time. In fact they were so advanced that they were good enough to serve as wards in the animal hospital run in conjunction with the Veterinary Science School set up at Langford House by Bristol University when it bought the property, very many years later – and they are still being used today.

Hill died, following a fall in his home, on 3rd March 1908. His body was conveyed in the carriage in which he always went to church and travelled the countryside and was pulled by his favourite bay horse. His funeral service was attended by so many mourners that the Methodist Church at Churchill could not contain them all and the funeral service was held outside, with interment alongside his wife in the mausoleum that he had built for her 27 years earlier in 1881.

Such was the popularity of Simon Sidney Hill in the area that postcards of the funeral were produced showing the very large number of mourners and the mausoleum. The Stan Croker postcard collection includes a card sent from Withey Cottage, Langford[17] describing the last wishes of Sidney Hill, "*He is to be buried at 2 o'clock on Tuesday with all the Sunday school children to follow. If fine, open air services at the chapel with tea being provided for 300 people coming from a distance. He is going to be taken in the waggonette as was his wish*".

Fig. 15 - The funeral of Simon Sidney Hill at Churchill
(Postcard David Lock collection, copy in BLHS Archives)

Hill was succeeded at Langford House by his nephew, Mr T. Sidney Hill, who inherited his uncle's fortune. He too became a generous benefactor and prominent in district and county public life.

Acknowledgements

The sources for the above account of the Christian life and work of Mr Simon Sidney Hill were taken from the excellent notes and records kept by Mrs Jean Darby – archivist of the Methodist Churches in the Banwell Circuit in North Somerset – and my debt to her is considerable. Also my thanks are due to Jennie Roberts for assistance in photographing Langford House, Langford, formerly the home of Simon Sidney Hill and now the University of Bristol's School of Veterinary Medicine.

My thanks are also due to Mr Jeffrey Spittal, the librarian and keeper of the extensive records and library that are held in John Wesley's Chapel, the New Room, in the Horsefair, Bristol. I am indebted to him for his time and patience in helping me to find answers to my many questions concerning Wesley's Journals in regard to Blagdon and Wesley's influence in the surrounding villages and the South-West.

Also, my grateful thanks are due to Janet Henderson, librarian, and Mike Brealey, assistant librarian, who generously allowed me access to the splendid library at Wesley College, College Park Drive, Henbury Road, Bristol and drew my attention to the records, pamphlets and notes that have been carefully preserved in their archives.

I acknowledge my great debt to those Blagdon Methodists who have kept alive the Methodist tradition during our time here, especially to the late Roy Taviner (former Clerk to the Parish Council) and Mrs Maureen Taviner and their family, Francis Parsons, George and Ruth Symes, Tony and Margaret Williams, David and Elaine Symes, Chris and Marion Ball, Margaret Edwards, Mrs Pip Riley and her late husband Colin, the late Nurse Lye, the late Mr & Mrs Burgess, and Dorothy and Patrick Eavis (brother of Micheal Eavis of Pilton and the Glastonbury Music Festival). I am sure there are other villagers I have inadvertently omitted to mention, but to all those Methodist ministers and local preachers who have toiled ceaselessly in their work for the Methodist Church in Blagdon: they have not laboured in vain.

Thanks also to Mr & Mrs Alan Barwick for a copy of their Indenture of Chapel Grove Court, and to David and Ann Lock's archive. My thanks are due to Mr Stan Croker for his permission to quote from the description of the arrangments for Mr Hill's funeral, written on the back of a postcard from his published collection.

Bibliography and Sources

Darby, Jean, Archivist of the Methodist Church in North Somerset Notes and Records. BLHS archive. Dissenter's letter August 6th 1805.

Mr & Mrs Alan Barwick Indenture 7th Nov. 1907 (BLHS archive)

Blagdon School log (1880-1918)

Croker, Stan *Picture Postcards of the early 1900s, The Wrington Vale* (self published, 2005)

Fryer, Jo, editor, et al *Every House Tells a Story* (Langford History Group, 2006)

Hey, David, *The Oxford Companion to Local and Family History* (OUP & BCA, 1996).

Hibbs, John, *The Country Chapel* (David and Charles, 1988)

Leary, William, *My Ancestors were Methodists*, 2nd ed. (Society of Genealogists, 1990).

Moorman., J.R.H., *A History of the Church in England* (A. & C. Black, 1953)

Pevsner, Nikolaus, *The Buildings of England: North Somerset and Bristol* (Penguin, 1958).

Waller, Ralph, *John Wesley* (SPCK, 2003).

Wesley, John, *Journals*, no.20 from September 4th 1782 to June 28th 1786

Wesley, John, *Works*, vol. 1, vol. 4, vol. 11, vol. 14, vol. 20.

Pamphlet *Welcome to the New Room, John Wesley's Chapel 1739*

References

[1]   William Leary, *My Ancestors were Methodists*, pp.4–5.

[2]   David Hay, *The Oxford Companion to Local and Family History*, p.227

[3]   Nikolas Pevsner, *The Buildings of England, North Somerset and Bristol*, p.110.

[4]   Leary, ibid, pp.4–5.

[5]   Pevsner, ibid, p.412.

[6]   Pamplet, *Welcome to the New Room, 'John Wesley's Chapel 1739'*, p.1.

[7]   Wesley's *Works*, vol.1, p.477.

[8]   ibid, vol.11, p.7.

[9]   ibid, vol. 14, p.399.

[10] ibid, vol. 20, p.191.

[11] ibid, vol. 4, p.192.

[12] ibid, vol.20, p.237.

[13] ibid, vol. 20, p.237.

[14] ibid, vol. 14, p.394.

[15] BLHS archive, Dissenter's letter dated August 6th 1805.

[16] BLHS archive, Barwick indenture dated 7th November 1907.

[17] Stan Croker, *Picture Postcards of the early 1900s, Wrington Vale*, p. 53.

Charles Wesley (1707-1788), John Wesley's younger brother, wrote over 5,500 hymns, words and music.

All photographs are by the author, except were otherwise noted.

The photograph of Langford House (c.1850) was by permission of the administrator. The photograph of a painting of the Reverend John Wesley M.A. was taken from a reproduction in the Minister's Vestry at Blagdon Methodist Church.

Teazles

Anne King

"The Uncles went down Curry Rivel way after harvest, loaded up the wagons with teazles and took them to Yorkshire."

I heard this, but was never sure when it happened, as these "Uncles" could be from any generation. My aunt Lil told me how she remembered uncle William, a very old man, coming from West Hatch to her uncle Henry Baker's funeral at Blagdon in 1908. She said his black coat was somewhat green with age and she never forgot his gnarled hands! Now that I am at the age of William when he made his sad journey home, this time perhaps by rail (for Blagdon by then had a passenger service from the main line at Yatton), my retirement has given me time to look back, and a visit to West Hatch church showed William's grave-stone with his correct age. He was born in Blagdon in 1832 and died in West Hatch in 1912 aged 80.

From registers, censuses and parish records preserved at the Somerset Record Office we found William was one of eight village boys attending the school at Blagdon — presumably through Baynard's Charity. By 1851 William, aged 18, was the eldest boy living at home in Sladacre Lane with his parents, but in 1855 he was married at West Hatch church to Charlotte Vickery, daughter of witness Joseph, a labourer of West Hatch. The other witness at the wedding was Isaac Hawkins from Compton Martin, who a few months later married Mary Vickery, sister of Charlotte. William and Charlotte, with their increasing family, lived and farmed at West Hatch, then Curland, Beer Crocombe and back to West Hatch by 1901, generally listed as "dairyman and teazle farmer." In 1881 at least three of their sons were teazle workers. There were other men from Blagdon, some from Ubley and Compton Martin, and a very few from Harptree, Chew Stoke or Wrington. Almost all were working on the teazle crop, which was very labour intensive.

There were two particular areas in the south west where teazle growing was so successful and both were in Somerset. Blagdon and Ubley formed the nucleus of the north Somerset region, whilst North Curry, Fivehead, Hatch Beauchamp, West Hatch, Curry Mallett and Isle Brewers could be described as the West Sedgemoor or south Somerset region. This shared specialist activity partly accounts for the interchange of population between these widely separated areas, for at the time of the census in 1851 at least 19 men from Blagdon or Ubley were working in the south

Somerset teazle fields. This trend continued, with many going south for regular work, marrying and settling into their own homes.

Isaac Caple, a teazle dealer from Blagdon, was often at West Hatch and by 1881 he had retired there. Three of the Young family were around Fivehead; they did not all stay, but John Young, who married locally, was farming 120 acres at Isle Brewers by 1881, whilst William Greenslade was at West Hatch with his wife from Oake. Edmund Addicott and William and Thomas Bath were at North Curry in 1851. Later Edmund and his wife were teazle growers and keeping a shop at West Hatch, William Bath was married and at West Hatch too, with Thomas lodging nearby. Four of the Derrick family, two Harris's, William Gallop, a Stephens, a Wyatt, a Baker and an Allen, all from the Blagdon area, were lodging with local families. A Thomas Clark from Litton was at West Hatch in 1861. In 1881 William Bath and his wife from Stoke St Gregory are living at Isle Brewers. They have their eight year old grandson, Francis Clarke from Blagdon, with them.

Among those returning to Blagdon with south Somerset wives were Thomas and Elizabeth Brunt, George and Mary Rayson, and Ephraim and Emma Wheeler, whilst Frank White from Hatch Beauchamp was living with the Shipsey family at Yoxter.

Fig. 1- Fuller's Teazles (John L Jones)

Early history

We sometimes see teazles on waste land or in gardens, usually the common teazle, a rough prickly plant with many spikey heads and growing about six feet high. The commercial variety, the Fuller's Teazle, similar, but with little hooks on the end of each spike, has stronger narrower heads. From time immemorial these have been used in the woollen industry for their combing effect. Our name comes from an Anglo-Saxon word "taesan" meaning "to tease cloth" and, as the Old English word was "taesel", the name has scarcely changed, although there are several different spellings still used today.

The London Record Society publish some customs accounts of 1480 which reveal ships sailing into London with thousands of teazles, most probably sent by Dutch traders. Sometimes these were packed in "pipes" or "baskets", or often in "skives." Duty payable appeared to be 6d a skive and a pipe was thought to contain 62 times as many teazles as a skive. With handling costs as well, it would have been very expensive to buy from abroad, and therefore not surprising that teazles became much grown in Essex and later in the West Country.

An early reference to a weaving industry around our area is in the local charity set up by the will of Blagdon-born Timothy Parker in 1681. He had become a successful "mercer" who exported a great deal of cloth from Bristol, where there was a thriving trade with Spain and with Ireland. His gift bought land known as Thomas's tenement, and this investment was to provide eight poor Blagdon widows with bread after church every Sunday. It was a needed and valued bequest in those hard times. Possibly he encouraged teazle growing and preparation of wool for weaving in Blagdon.

As more land was used for teazles in Somerset, disputes arose about the paying of tithes. The lawful arrangement was for the 'lay owner' of the farm land to receive 'Great Tithes', that is, money for every crop of corn, hay, etc., and the vicar to receive 'Small Tithes', which included livestock, milk, poultry and garden produce. The new crop caused confusion about who should receive this tithe and eventually (quoting from J.H. Bettey's account of proceedings'):

"A commission was appointed to enquire into the matter, and met at the Sign of the Golden Lyon in Wrington on 13th April 1699. The commissioners were John Freke, William Sherston and John Knight. The numerous witnesses included the incumbents of Wrington, Cheddar, Christon, Compton Bishop, Churchill, Yatton and Brockley. All agreed that the cultivation of teazles had greatly increased throughout the district during the previous thirty or forty years, and that they were now extensively grown in the district, but there was no unanimity as to how the tithes were levied. Most witnesses, however, took the view that they were 'small tithes' and properly belonged to the incumbent. A few even suggested, quite illogically, that since the teazle seeds were so small the crop could not be other than 'small tithe'.

"Some witnesses gave details of the method of cultivation: Anne Cooke of Congresbury, widow, aged 67, and Richard Symons of Churchill, gentleman, aged 65, both described how teazles were generally sown on newly-broken pasture land or on land where wheat had previously been grown. The seed was sown in March or April, and the teazles were transplanted in the autumn or the following spring. By St James's tide (25 July) they were usually ready for harvest and were cut with knives and 'gathered in handfuls, the best first, the middlings next, and the small last, all in the same season.' They were evidently a profitable crop, and John Balton of Wrington, yeoman, aged 60, stated that 'a good acre of teazles is as good or rather better than a good acre of wheate.'

"Lewis Wathell of Congresbury, husbandman, aged 55, stated that the cultivation of teazles had increased greatly during his lifetime and that there were now more than eighty acres sown each year in the parish. He claimed that the crop had been introduced about 45 years previously by John Eke who had brought teazle seeds from Cheddar and sown them in his garden.

"Clearly the rapid increase in the acreage devoted to the crop deprived the lay impropriators of the tithe they might otherwise have levied on wheat or barley which could have been grown on the same land. Several witnesses pointed out, however, that teazles were an advantage for impropriators, since because they were usually grown on newly-broken pasture or meadow land, where wheat or other grain was later sown, they increased the amount of arable land. They also served to deprive the incumbents of the tithes of milk, cheese and livestock. No conclusion to this dispute has been found but there can be no doubt of its importance in the district."

Years later the high cost of teazles caused the clothiers to attempt to reduce prices. They blamed speculators for forcing prices up. Meetings were held at which they considered importing cheaper teazles, probably from Holland. In the same year Robert Clark of Blagdon died, and the 1772 entry in the burial register[2] shows that the Vicar was aware of these problems, for he wrote, "This man acquired a handsome fortune by speculating in teazles, buying them at a guinea and keeping them 'til they sold for five guineas."

How the teazles were used

Children have sometimes been shown how to collect sheep's wool, and, holding a teazle in each hand, to comb the fibres. This is the first stage when preparing wool for spinning, and the common teazle could be used. They could be fixed on to little wooden hand-held frames, called cards, perhaps because the Latin name for teazle was "cardus". The process of cleaning and straightening raw wool is called "carding".

A local experienced carder and spinner feels that teazles would never have been strong enough to cope with this process, and that the later wire cards would have been a most welcome development. In very early days people made the best of what was available and the family would have had to spend many tedious hours working. Arkwright's carding machine of leather and wires around a cylinder gradually replaced hand carding in the 19th century. There was an important trade in hand cards to the wool trade all over England, with many workers employed. Cards were usually supplied with the wool to the spinners. Many teazles would be used in this way.

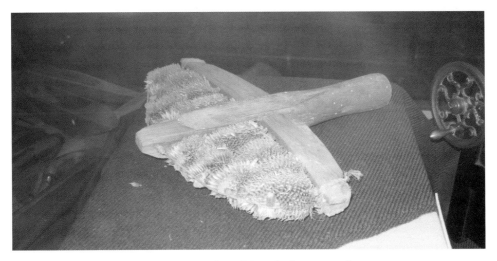

Fig. 2 - Hand Card (Trowbridge Museum)

After wool had been carded, cleaned, spun, dyed and woven, and so many complex processes completed, the better cloths were skilfully worked on for many hours, with teazles being used to raise the nap. For this the heads were tightly packed in large frames drawn across the cloth by hand.

New machines were gradually being introduced. In the late 1700s one was the "gig-mill", where many teazle heads were fitted into bars which rotated continuously on the cloth. All these labour-saving methods were bitterly resented by the workers, and resulted in riots, unemployment and increasing poverty, especially amongst home workers. Much more power was needed and fewer workers were employed, but this more extravagant use of the heads must have been helpful to Blagdon's economy!

Fig. 3 - Teazle Gig (Trowbridge Museum)

Between 2,500 and 4,000 teazle heads were needed to set up one gig drum, which consisted of 24 long frames or double rods, with just space for the teazle head to be compressed between. Heads were fitted all along the length of the rod (maybe six feet), and this choosing and fitting was very skilled work. When set, the rods were fitted around the gig drum to rotate at speed against the cloth moving in the opposite direction. As the little hooks wore away the pressure and speed of the gig could be altered. One wrongly-sized teazle could leave a permanent streak on the entire length of cloth, one Huddersfield teazle fitter told me. Another stressed that they made the best cloth in the world — and it couldn't be done without teazles. The feeling in Yorkshire today in favour of teazles is still so strong that there must have been great antagonism to mechanical substitutes. There was pride that the best manufacturers did not lower their standards.

Teazles picked up moisture from the very damp cloth. A handle-house with some form of ventilation was necessary near a cloth-workers' workshop for drying the teazles. On the Wells side of Shepton Mallet, Darshill House has an adjoining handle-house still easily recognisable. The stream flowing close by provided water power for several mills along its length.

Fig. 4 - The Handle-house near Croscombe.
(author's photograph)

Cultivation and harvesting

Two pecks of seeds per acre were sown in March, either in well-spaced rows or broadcast. Horse-hoeing or hand weeding and thinning was necessary. In Fivehead, "The plants would then be pulled and put into piles to await being carted away by horse and putt, a small almost square cart, to the area where they were planted for their permanent life. The planting had to be finished by Christmas and they would still be kept weed-free if possible till the following July/August when the teazles would have formed and bloomed, the flowers covering the whole of the head with a pale mauve haze."

A density of 16,000 plants on an acre was aimed for. The strong tap-root of the plant broke up hard soil and took its nourishment deeper than most crops, but this helped prepare the land for wheat. "The crop drew so much goodness from the ground that it could only be grown in the same patch once in seven years." A long narrow spade was skilfully used for all work around the plants until the following spring. In this area the work was called "spudling". The many hours needed for spudling gave rise to our local saying, "just spudling about", which could be applied to someone taking too long on a job.

As the petals dropped, the heads were ready for picking. The largest heads, the kings, came first, followed later by middlings, and a last cut of the smaller "scrubs" a week or two later.

Fig. 5 - The Teazle Field (John L Jones)

Harvesting was prolonged and uncomfortable and the weather had to be dry. The cutter had to reach upwards for many of the heads, so it was tiring work, and hot, because a strong old coat had to be worn as protection from prickles and the strong black juice from the stems which spoiled clothing and was poisonous to cut fingers.

Gloves made of horse leather were needed, and a small curved knife, often made from an old scythe blade, was tied to the right hand glove. A West Sedgemoor vestry book tells how, in 1787 a distressed parishioner was provided with gloves and a hook to let him work. He received 2/3 for a pair of horse leather gloves for teazling.

Fig. 6 - Gloved Hand (John L Jones)

*Fig. 7 - Handful of Teazles
(Martin George)*

Mrs Phyllis Tapp of Curry Mallet, who had cut teazles, said that it was a horrible prickly, tiring job, ruined your clothes, and was very bad on the hands. The teazles were collected in handfuls of 40 or 50. One with a stem cut longer than the usual eight inches was put among the bunch and wrapped around the short stems to bond them securely together. The handfuls, left in heaps along the rows, were collected by children in the evenings and handed to the cutters to be lugged.

All the handfuls were attached to the long poles — lugs — which were leant against a wooden framework or "gallows" if the weather was dry, and carried to open sheds if rain threatened. The filled lugs were heavy. "An average acre might yield 200,000 heads", said a grower in south Somerset.[3]

Fig. 8 - Filling the Lug (John L Jones)

A Huddersfield pattern designer working in the mid-1900s tells of 26 gigs all busy in one mill. The produce of one acre would last such a mill for three settings of its gigs, and teazles would last the 17 hours needed for a really good quality cloth from Dobroyd.

Most mills obtained their teazles from the specialising factors who bought from the growers and used their own premises for trimming, grading and often setting. Edmund Taylor, teazle merchant, was the most well known, and buyers I have spoken with remember visits to Somerset and France. There are happy memories of gatherings with growers and colleagues, and bookings being made at a Taunton hotel. Here are echoes of the Blagdon dealers when they visited Sedgemoor years ago.

Figure 9 - The Full Lugs – left out to dry in good weather (John L Jones)

There must have been very many of these long straight poles not needed in winter and spring, and the Blagdon Vestry minute books contain references to teazle lugs being borrowed when the church was in need of repair – it seems for scaffolding. At home we always had one or two long poles which we called lugs, and they were used then to knock down cider apples. Ten feet was often the standard length. Tall straight young trees must have been grown particularly for lugs as each grower would have so many in use at the same time. The staving mentioned later would have enabled the growers to keep lugs and send teazles off neatly packed on shorter stakes.

In 1813, Blagdon dealer and grower James Capel paid an extraordinary price for "The Field", four acres, nos. 378 and 382 on the tithe map, known until recently as Mr Wood's field, on the hill slope between Score and Sladacre Lanes. It had road access and may already have had a brick-built open shed, probably for keeping teazles dry (*fig. 10*). The way the older low stone building had been extended with the new roof line giving increased height is significant. It has been said that a good teazle crop could pay for the land it grew on! Thirty years later this field had changed ownership and was pasture being used by William Derrick.

Fig. 10 - This building had good headroom for the teazle lugs.

Trading

After the drying season, about September or early October, buyers would come to examine the crop, as the teazles were used in the manufacture of good quality cloth to bring up the "nap", and usually the seller was given a suit-length of cloth from the mills. After a sale was agreed large sheets would be sent to pack the teazles in. The Victoria County History describes the next process", the handfuls were undone, and seeds for next year's crop shaken out, before all heads were carefully graded and re-tied".[4] They were then fastened around shorter "staves" or staffs in circular fashion.

From the picture the stave looks over 2ft long, and the diameter less. This stave may be the 'skive' which was mentioned in 1480. The staves were said to carry thirty handfuls, and thirty staves made a pack. As teazles were sold by the pack, I guess these were rolled in one sheet, and made a suitable length to carry on horse-drawn farm wagons. In later years handfuls were sent in the sheets to avoid the extra work of staving.

Fig. 11 - A Stave (Royal Bath & West Society)

For the more local mills such as Frome, Wiltshire or Gloucestershire, the wagons were loaded and made the whole journey. Billingsley, in his report, writes about teazles going to Wiltshire, and also that "Large quantities are also sent by water conveyance from Bristol into Yorkshire".[5] If teazles were sent from Bristol by sea there should be records, but so far I have found none, just two instances of ships carrying teazles to Ireland in 1801 and 1817. Journeys by sea at that time were so slow.

The West of England broad-cloth was selling well and in very great demand. Transport of goods in bulk was always expensive and difficult. Pack-horses were replaced by wheeled vehicles as soon as roads were firmer. The improvement came from the turnpike trusts, so that stagecoach journeys were better (although Bath to London coaches had been possible earlier.) Inns were able to feed and rest many horses a day, for all road transport depended on them. Around 1800 Telford made roads to bear a heavy wagon, and in 1815 MacAdam was surveyor-general of Bristol roads. Surprisingly, imported wool was brought to Wiltshire by wagons from the major ports. There were large carrier businesses – Claveys at Frome were well known (this is still a local name) – so it seems possible that wagons were travelling from Somerset to Yorkshire. Finished cloths were sent long distances, often to London factors. In spite of the risks of mishaps and robberies there were many wealthy merchants.

Enquiries at Manchester, Kingston upon Hull, and around Yorkshire found no evidence of teazles arriving from Bristol at all. A leaflet found at Bristol with price lists for imports to Hull showed what the charge would be if teazles were among the cargo to be unloaded at the port in 1842. In the Middle Ages, and perhaps later, teazles had been imported from the continent. Charges for landing, wharfage and housing in 1842 had been about 2/- per vat or large crate, but in 1846 there was a change to charging by the long package – for example, 30ft and under, 31–50ft, 51–80ft, 81ft and upwards, with only the latter paying the rate formerly charged for crates. Was there an attempt to lower prices because of the looming threat from fast and cheap rail transport which would soon capture the trade? Living memory from Fivehead is that "The packed sheets were loaded on to wagons and taken to the nearest GWR station for the start of their long journey North."

The late John Millar and Beryl were researching teazles before John so sadly died. They found the names of dealers John Bailey, Ralph Hemans and William Derrick were all on early 19th century deeds of their house and others around Bell Square. John wrote that the land between the church and the west side of the village was used by these dealers, and that they "shipped" teazles to Frome by horse and cart. This is an interesting use of the word which has come to be used for any method of transporting goods. Would it often have been used for carting? Is this how teazles were "shipped" from Bristol? Alternatively, Blagdon men may have taken teazles to Bristol, bound for Yorkshire, and the story as it passed down lost the "to Bristol" reference. Teazles would have been taken all the way by wagon after the improvement of the roads, but before there was good rail transport.

Although Blagdon must have been a thriving village with good employment there were hard times too. In 1822 Eliza Boulton applied for parish relief. She was allowed

4/- weekly, "on condition that her teazles growing on The Wood Piece become the property of the parish until she re-imburses them". Her son Robert Boulton, one of the men serving for Blagdon in 1797 to prevent Napoleon's invasion, had returned home and probably worked on the land. He was industrious, for in 1822 he received 5/6 second poor money (which only went to those not on parish relief). His death that year left Eliza destitute and we can only hope that she benefited from a good harvest. She died seven years later aged 79. The Wood Piece may have been no.584 or 595 in the Garston area. The first was four acres of arable and the second a one acre pasture at the time of the 1842 tithe map.

The crop depended on good weather. That, and the state of trade, made prices per pack variable. A pack would contain 9,000 kings or 20,000 midlings at a time when John Billingsley said 15-16 packs per acre, whilst later on D. Rowe said 7-10. Known prices per pack are: 1700, £6 (when wages were 6/- weekly); 1790s average £2; 1810-20 often £20 (boom after Napoleonic wars); 1829, £2 10/-; 1900s, £20 according to season.

Blagdon farmer John Challenger in 1842 owned Fir Tree Farm and other houses and land including the Garston area and the Cawkerds. The family were farming it all themselves and by 1851 John is described as a teazle dealer too.

So many Blagdon residents settled and stayed in south Somerset in the second half of the 19th century that it must have been for the better opportunity to use their specialised skills. The death of 95 year old Mrs Louisa Wilkins is recorded in the Blagdon parish magazine of 1913. She had said "how she regretted no teasles being grown as they employed so many people." It is not clear why Blagdon ceased teazling half a century before Fivehead. Billingsley reported some problems, obviously not too serious. Much later, wire-worm was suspected, but later still, investigation isolated eel-worm as a major pest. The southern areas were still teazling when modern pest control could combat this problem. It was also found that long field rests did not kill the eel-worm due to crops of oats, mangolds, beans, and hedgerow plants cleavers and chickweed perpetuating its life-cycle.

There are so few memories now of family relationships. On a visit to Curry Mallet we were lucky, quite by chance, to meet a lady who remembered harvesting teazles herself and she told us her maiden name was Derrick! We found her very interested in our story, and happy for us to find her a family link with our area if possible, but had never heard of it herself. A few teazles were still being grown there after the last war. Very fortunately, Mrs Phyllis Tapp gave us the names of her grandfather and father and told us where she had lived, and we were able to trace her descent from Blagdon.

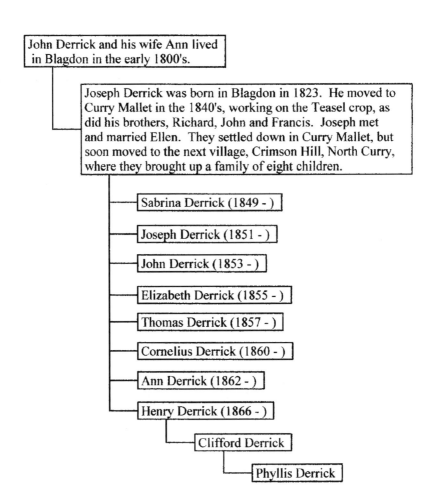

From Blagdon to Yorkshire ...

As the Yorkshire woollen industry grew due to its advantage of coal-produced steam power, the west of England mills gradually lost trade. More teazles than before were needed in the north, and British teazle heads were preferred for their greater strength.

There were several unsettled years of Napoleonic war around 1800, with massed armies — nearly 50,000 men from Somerset, including at least twelve from Blagdon (Vestry proceedings D/P Blagdon 13/2/2) — well used to marching from the south-west to Portsmouth, Dover, Colchester, even York. Always there were baggage wagons and equipment to accompany the foot soldiers. Those returning men, like Robert Boulton, were knowledgeable and confident travellers experienced in making long journeys and it could be wrong to under-estimate their influence in the village.

Isaac Baker (b.1778) was also away from the village during these years. His wife Ann and his son William are shown on censuses to be from East Bergholt on the Essex/Suffolk border, an area of many small harbours, and also near Colchester and the north road. William (b.1803), Isaac and Ann were in Blagdon by 1808 when daughter Harriet was christened. I do not know why Isaac was at the east coast but he may have been in the army or navy. This family remained in Blagdon in old age. The West Hatch William was a grandson of Isaac.

Early registers and the 1841 census, taken in June that year, show few Blagdon men living in Sedgemoor, but for years they may have been making annual visits, after their own harvest, to load up and carry teazles. Did the dealers send wagons down with local men prepared to take seasonal work and bring back loads as they returned? How far did they take the loads? Did they drive further than Bristol and complete the deliveries? The Yorkshire archive services have all been most helpful with my inquiries but have found no references to teazles arriving at the mills. Continued research may one day discover the answer to this question, but I now accept that Blagdon men did make this journey with teazles from the home area to Yorkshire, and that the most likely years would have been 1800-1860.

Almost a postscript!

Martin, the son of Cyril George, a director of Edmund Taylor & Son of Huddersfield, the leading and last working teazle merchant, remembers coming with his father by Land Rover and trailer to buy teazles from Park Farm in the Curry Rivel area and take them back to their premises. They had hoped to encourage more acreage, but the crops needed too much labour. So the last loads of Somerset teazles did go by road, and he was pleased to say the same large sheets were used until the end. The sheets were about 15ft square, hessian, folded and stitched up the side. Never called bags, they were open ended and had strong wooden pins to close the ends, which needed the force of a knee to fasten them.

When the teazles arrived in Huddersfield, this was the destination. The modern premises of Edmund Taylor are shown here with a family member who is described as the last of the teazle workers. It has been a privilege to be told about their work by very skilled men justly proud of all that was achieved, and so sorry for its demise.

Telephone 2375

EDMUND TAYLOR (Teazle) Ltd.,
Teazle Merchants,
CHARDON MILL,
CARR PIT ROAD, MOLDGREEN
HUDDERSFIELD

Fig. 12 - Closing Memories (Tim Ledger)

Fig. 13. – Teazle raising machine (gig) Tomlinson's Ltd Rochdale
(John Schofield)

This gig was made by Tomlinson's of Rochdale in the first half of the 20th century, and remained in use much later than the Trowbridge gig of the west of England cloth trade. Over 20 of these were in use at the same time at Dobroyd in Yorkshire which specialized in cashmere and other expensive fancy woolens. Their buyers came to Taunton, met the growers and selected the teazles best for their uses. At the mill they were trimmed, graded and set. Setting was very skilled work – "it was magical to watch the setter putting them in by feel" said the designer.[6] Dobroyd sadly closed in the 1970s.

References:

1. Dr J.H. Bettey, *The Cultivation of Teazles in North Somerset, Somerset and Dorset Notes and Queries 1998,* p.235.
2. D/P/blag/2/1/6 *Baptisms and Burials 1766-1807,* Somerset Record Office, (transcription in BLHS archives) p.14.
3. John L. Jones, *The Teazle Harvest in Somerset,* published in Somerset and Wessex Life, Nov. 1973, p.46.
4. *Victoria County History, Book 2,* p542-3.
5. John Billingsley, *Agricultural Survey of Somersetshire,* p.110.
6. Author's personal communication with Mr George Howell – the late Mr Barrett was the teazle setter and foreman whom he valued so much.

Bibliography - much enjoyed publications.

1. Acland, T.D. & Sturge, W. *The Farming of Somerset.* J. Murray, 1851.
2. Albert, W. *The Turnpike road system in England.* Cambridge University Press, 1972
3. *Bath and West Society Journal* (particularly the stave) 1937/8.
4. Billingsley, J. *General view of the agriculture of the county of Somerset.* 1798.
5. *Directory & gazetteer of Somerset and Bristol* 1872
6. Edwards, P. *Rural Life.* Batsford, 1993.
7. Fisher, W.G. *History of the Somerset Yeomanry.* Goodman & Son, 1924.
8. Fivehead Parish *Map Committee Press,* 1999.
9. Jones, J.L. *The Teasel harvest in Somerset etc.*
10. Kermode, J. *Medieval merchants of York, Beverly and Hull.* Cambridge University Press, 1998.
11. Mann, J. de L. *The Cloth industry in the West of England, 1640-1880,* Oxford University Press, 1971.
12. Millar, J. *The Teazlers.* Blagdon and Charterhouse Parish Magazine Archive BLHS.
12. Rogers, K.H. *Warp and weft: the development and decay of the Somerset and Wiltshire woollen industry.* Barracuda, 1986.
14. *Victoria County History of the county of Somerset.* Constable, 1911. vol.2, p.542-3.

With grateful thanks for the kind help of:
Somerset Record Office and Somerset Mobile Library Service
Somerset & Dorset Notes & Queries: the Editor for permission to quote Dr Bettey
East Yorkshire and West Yorkshire Archive Services, York, Hull City Archives, Manchester Archives and Local Studies: who have all been unfailingly prompt and interested.
Somerset Studies Library for locating unknown sources.
Trowbridge Museum for its display and allowing photographs.
The Somerset Rural Life Museum, and Friends of the Abbey Barn
Bristol Record Office
Blagdon Local History Society archives and members.
Mrs D. Jones for generous help from her late husband,
John L. Jones's outstanding work.
Mrs P. Tapp for her friendship and memories.
Martin George, descendant of Edmund Taylor (Teazle) Ltd.
The Huddersfield Examiner, where my letter was read by so many people willing to share their special memories of skilled work.
Stewart Gledhill, amateur film club member for his teazle filming before it was too late.
Ted King for his work, interest and encouragement.

The Weavers' Milk Round

Mike Adams

Introduction

The Weavers were the last of the independent producer-retailers of untreated milk in Blagdon. Keith and his father Ernest delivered milk in Bristol for ten years until the air raids during World War Two made it impossible to continue. Keith, joined by his wife-to-be Ruth in 1947, had a pivotal role in Blagdon village life delivering their milk daily for 50 years – giving Keith a total of 60 years in the industry. The whole village celebrated their retirement at a function in Coombe Lodge in 1991. This article includes Keith's and Ruth's recollections of the daily routine on their farm, the milk round and the highs and lows of the dairy industry.

Lower Ellick Farm

Keith Weaver's family has lived around Mendip for many generations. Keith's father Ernest, born in 1883, was the son of Isaac and Jemima Weaver – one of ten children born at Hounsley Farm, Regil. As a young man Ernest worked with his father on the farm, but in 1910 he moved to Lower Ellick Farm at the top of Burrington Combe. The farm was part of the Wills Estate, rented from Lord Winterstoke, with the farmhouse and buildings on the Ham side of the road as well as 80 acres of farmland and buildings under Blackdown.

Fig. 1 - Sheep shearing prize

Ernest took with him about ten Dairy Shorthorn cattle and a couple of horses when he moved to Lower Ellick on his own. Later in 1910 he married Charlotte, 'Lottie', the daughter of Bill and Eliza Patch who ran the Crown Inn at Regil. She brought a pony and a cow, which were her father's marriage gift. Unfortunately her cow later died after falling over the rocks at the top of Burrington Combe. They also kept sheep, and Ernest became so competent at shearing that one year he won second prize at the Wrington Vale sheep shearing competition and was awarded a Silver Spirit tea pot (fig.1) and medal which the Weavers still own.

Fig. 2a – Aerial view of Lower Ellick Farm (rebuilt)

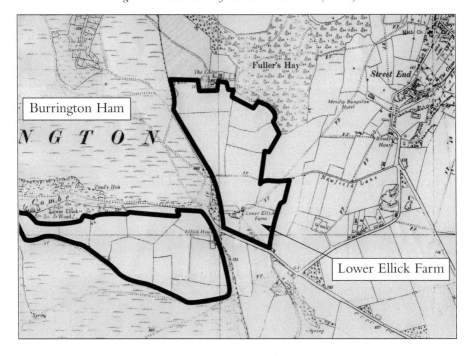

Fig. 2b – Location and size of Lower Ellick Farm (land outlined in black)

Lower Ellick Farm expanded to 120 acres when the neighbouring Ham Farm relinquished its land. The new tenancy extended their grazing rights on Burrington Ham, locally called 'The Ham' or sometimes 'The Common' because it is common land. Several commoners held these rights or 'stints' depending on which animals they kept: there were so many stints for sheep, cattle, geese etc.[1] The dry stone wall between both farms and the Ham marks the boundary between the parishes of Blagdon and Burrington (fig. 2a & 2b).

On Blackdown there was a lot of gorse and bracken which had to be cleared for grazing and later for ploughing. Keith remembers the host of wild flowers such as yellow rattle, green orchid, quaking grass and moon daisies in the permanent pastures.[2] With their commoner's rights, Keith's father Ernest and Edwin Carpenter were able to go up on Blackdown to cut bracken for bedding using a single horse mower, and sometimes Edwin is thought to have used a scythe. Keith recalled:

'It was a bad place to cut. Taking wagons up to load, it was so awkward that many times he's toppled them over. The bracken was used as bedding because the area grew little corn at that time – what went for bedding usually was fusty hay.'[3]

Ernest and Lottie developed a truly mixed farm with over 200 hens providing eggs for sale and roasting chickens for Christmas. They also kept pigs. Each year one was killed for eating, some was eaten fresh, the rest was preserved by salting in a long lead-lined trough. As a Wills tenant Ernest was allowed to take part in regular rabbit shoots organised by the estate. Keith remembers riding up on to Blackdown and seeing the uncultivated land near Charterhouse seething with rabbits. The rabbits were considered to be a menace, and needed to be controlled. Ernest also used to snare rabbits for sale at market.

In addition to the farm work Lottie used to take in paying guests, including some TB patients and visitors to Nordrach Sanatorium – she used to say she made more money that way than they did from farming. A Mrs Ingram and her daughter Audrey, who was a TB patient, stayed long-term.

Keith's early years

In 1915 Gwendoline May was the first child to be born to Ernest and Lottie, and Ernest Keith arrived 2½ years later in 1918 (fig. 16). Keith and Gwen attended Blagdon school, over a mile away from Lower Ellick Farm, and they both walked to school along Luver's Lane, down The Rhoddy, then The Rocks and The Grove path to the main road and along to the school.[4] At this time the school had about 100 pupils, with John Westbrook as head master. Keith was a hardworking student and did well in the 'three Rs' – reading, writing and 'rithmetic.

On Wednesdays the boys worked in the school garden (fig. 3) with Mr Westbrook or Mr Johnson, and they were allowed to take home what they grew. The school garden was situated on the site of East Croft Close and it had its own well. After school Keith had violin lessons with Sid Bolton in the 'Live and Let Live' pub opposite the school.

Fig. 3 – Blagdon school gardening class, Keith is in the middle of the back row

On Sundays Gwen and Keith would go to Sunday school at the Baptist Chapel in Blagdon, or to the one at Rickford Hall run by Miss Annie Heaven. As teenagers the Weavers joined the Young Farmers which used to meet each week in the John Locke room in Wrington or at Farrington Gurney.

Keith left school at the age of 14 to work on the farm and help his father with the milk round.

The Fire

Coming home from school on 6th March 1931 Keith found Lower Ellick farm house had been devastated by fire. The fire started at about 9 o'clock in the morning, when the chimney caught fire, and soon spread to the roof. It was thought that burning soot got into the valley between the roofs which melted the lead on the roof, spreading the fire very quickly (figs. 4, 5 & 6).

**_Lower Ellick farmhouse
was devastated by fire in
March 1931_**

*Fig. 4 - Lower Ellick farm house
in 1930, note the windows, porch
and lean-to on the right*

*Fig. 5 - After the fire in 1931,
the porch is intact*

*Fig. 6 - The re-built farm house with enlarged
windows and the porch and lean-to preserved*

*'It started in the roof and we
ended up with nothing whatever
upstairs and not a lot downstairs
... the house had a double gable,
with lead guttering through the
centre. I know there was a chimney
fire in the morning and we
understood it was a lump of soot
which fell down on the guttering.'.'*

The fire engine broke down coming up Burrington Combe on its way to the fire; it would have come from Sandford or Winscombe.

"Nothing was saved except a wooden chest, no clothes, nothing. When Keith came back from school that day all he had were the clothes he stood up in. Sadly, they had no insurance so they had to start from scratch again. Mr Austin, who was a paying guest, gave the family £25, but otherwise they had nothing. The Wills family rebuilt the house and it had to be on the same foundations, retaining the original porch and lean-to. It took a couple of years to be rebuilt by Milliars of Rickford. Meanwhile the family went to live at 'Chalet Ponti' on Ellick Road and at Ham Farm Cottage."[5]

Milk round in Bristol 1931–41

Originally all milk was taken from the farm by pony and trap to Burrington Station on the Wrington Vale Light Railway[6] to catch the milk train to Bristol (fig. 16). Later it was collected by lorry.

'Nestles (Anglo-Swiss Condensed Milk Co) used to pick up the milk from each farm. Before them, it was a Bristol firm called Case. The Nestles 10-gallon milk churns were heavy steel and had a brass plate with the individual farmer's name.'

Eventually this collection became uneconomic because of poor prices and Ernest decided to try his luck retailing the milk himself.

'We started a milk round in 1931, just after the house burnt down. We had 10 years in Bristol. At that time, there was a complete slump in agriculture again. For winter milk in October 1931 all we'd get was 3½d per gallon. We had to do something so we started the milk round in Bristol'.

John Gallop, a local farmer, added, *'It was about the time my grandmother started a round in Blagdon, which was subsequently sold to E. Weaver & Son in the 1940s soon after her death. At one time there were several small milk rounds in Blagdon.'*

"First of all we had leaflets printed and canvassed an area of Bristol – Cotham, Clifton and Redland to start with. Every morning after first milking, Keith and his dad would drive the 15 miles into Bristol with churns of milk, measuring cans and ladles going door-to-door to sell their milk.[7] People then came to the door with their jugs which were filled from the churn. Later on in the 1930s milk was bottled on the farm in wide-necked bottles with cardboard disc tops and there were two vans delivering in Bristol."

Fig. 7 - Keith in the dairy wearing his familiar hat; bottling machinery on the right

Fig. 8 - A selection of bottles normally kept inside the Weavers' porch. The two pint bottles, front left, are the oldest design with the wider neck for a cardboard top. The five pint bottles on the right take the aluminium top. Rear left is a half-pint bottle and the tallest is a quart (two pints) bottle which was most popular in Bristol

The two vans used to meet in the middle of their rounds and switch over milk if one was a bit short. The Weavers 'were one of the first in the district to have TT milk.' The first cardboard disc tops had to be put on by hand – that was before they had a bottling plant. An outline hole was punched into the top so that you could press it in to use a drinking straw. Keith still has some of the bottles at home now – they are really heavy, about twice the weight of a modern bottle (fig. 7 & 8). The bottles were made by Pilkington's, who also produced Pyrex glass. Even with the plant, the bottles had to be rinsed on revolving brushes and sterilised by hand – two at a time. Likewise they were attached to the bottling machine two at a time then handed on to a second person to press the lids on.

Fig. 9 - The first Austin delivery van, bought in 1931,
with Keith standing alongside and his father Ernest at the wheel.

'*There was a very bad winter in February 1940. Coming back across Broadfield Down, big telegraph poles were snapped off like matchsticks. The wires and even the grass were thick with ice. We carried on in Bristol until 1941. To start with, we did not get any bombing for almost a year. When the bombing started, if you were on the wrong side of the bridge at Hotwells, you had to stay in there. We spent several nights in the Rocks Railway tunnel. There were a lot of people in there as well – you were safe in there – more or less. One night we were at Bedminster Down and we looked back – all Bridge Street was a mass of flames. They used to drop incendiaries first and follow up with high explosive. It was a terrible time. A lot of people moved out of town to the countryside and several customers were killed, so we gave up in 1941 and concentrated on Blagdon and neighbouring villages.*'

Ruth comes to the West Country

Ruth Statham was born in November 1924 in Manchester (fig. 10), one of four children of whom only two survived to adulthood. When war broke out in September 1939, Ruth, aged 15¾, was on holiday with her aunt and cousin and on return to Manchester she found her school had been evacuated. Children like Ruth who had missed the evacuation remained at school part-time but had lots of homework. After taking her school certificate examinations Ruth left school and went to work in a shipping office. She knitted socks, balaclavas and scarves for the war effort, including a pair of mittens for her big brother.

On reaching the age of 17½ Ruth became liable for conscription or work in war-related industry and after reading an attractive poster: 'Join the Land Army, choose what you want to do and be posted close to home', she promptly volunteered. Ruth was soon called up to start her training at the Steambow Hostel near Pilton in Somerset. Facilities were very basic but they made their own fun – there were no phones in homes or hostels then, so they had to wait for letters to arrive bringing news of home. It was hard work but they had to stick it out.

At the beginning of 1943 Ruth was allowed home for a weekend and on 21st January she made the long trip from Manchester to Blagdon – the journey by rail and bus taking thirteen hours. And so Ruth began work as a land girl on Butcombe Farm with Mr and Mrs Stanley Roach.[8] She could hardly understand what the workers were saying in their broad Somerset accents and they had trouble understanding her Mancunian burr. They worked long hours with only half a day off each week from January to September, when Ruth had a week off to go home. In March 1944 the farm was sold to Mr and Mrs Tisdall and Ruth moved to Blagdon, lodging with Mr and Mrs Bill Lyons and cycling to and from work each day. Wages were £2 10s a week, out of which she had to pay for her lodgings and send money home to her mother. There wasn't much left over.

In 1947 Ruth left Butcombe Farm and went to live at 'Fairways' in Blagdon, close to Lower Ellick Farm where she began working in the dairy and on the milk round (fig. 11 & 12). 'Fairways' was built as a YWCA hostel for working women to enjoy the countryside at a very affordable price, in use both during and after the war.

Fig. 10 - Ruth aged about nine

*Fig. 12 - Ruth and Keith on the milk
van in 1947 outside Fairways YWCA.
Ruth is holding a quart bottle*

*Fig. 11 - Having a quick 'cuppa' in
land girl uniform at Fairways YWCA*

*Fig. 13 - Wedding Day 13th August 1949,
St Andrews Church, Blagdon*

The winter of 1947 was severe, with 10-foot snowdrifts in places.

"In 1947 the snow started when Ruth and Keith were out on the milk round. They had to abandon the van at the Rock of Ages and do the rest of the journey on foot arriving back at the farm looking like abominable snowmen! Ruth then had to trek across the fields to Fairways where she lived. The winds drove the snow into drifts, in places over 10 feet high, and over the tops of hedgerows … the snow lasted for many weeks. One night the milk van was the only vehicle able to go up Redhill while many others had been abandoned at the side of the road [possibly the weight of milk supplied grip on the road][9]. *Of course, in 1947 there were no snow ploughs and no salt on the roads so the snowdrifts had to be cleared manually."*

Ruth Statham and Keith Weaver became engaged in May 1947 and were married on 13th August 1949 at St Andrew's Church in Blagdon (fig. 13). It was a very warm sunny day and Blagdon Flower Show was taking place on The Mead. Dear Liverpudlian Pete Ryley, the village postman, took a week off work to run the milk round while Ruth and Keith were on honeymoon in Guernsey.

Keith and Ruth's first home was 'Greengates'[10] in Church Street, Blagdon. *"The house had 13 windows, 13 doors and 13 stairs which seemed like a good omen as they were married on the 13th."*

The second delivery van was used for family outings in the 1950s and 1960s – after being washed out with disinfectant and fitted with a blanket for everyone to sit on! It was a bit of a bumpy ride.

Keith's mother Lottie died in 1960 and when his father Ernest died in 1962, the family, including three young children, moved from 'Greengates' up to Lower Ellick Farm.

Milk round in Blagdon 1941-91

'When the bombing started, a land mine was dropped at the bottom of Blackdown. It came down on a silk parachute. I went up that morning and dragged back a piece of silk. It was a stupid thing to do and I got told off by the police.'

Ruth described the milk round as going down Station Hill in Blagdon to the top of Butcombe and back to Aldwick and Cowslip Green, on to Redhill where they reversed up the lane to Bill Lee's parents then crossing the A38 by the Darlington Arms to Lye Hole, then where Alvis's is now, on to Upper Langford, Burrington and back up Burrington Combe to their farm. In 1951 they gave up most of the round outside Blagdon except for Rickford, Burrington and Upper Langford.[11]

The first winter on the farm for Keith and Ruth and their three young children in 1962/3 was another memorable one.

"The snow started quietly on Christmas Eve and snowed all through the night. Once the wind got up the snow was blown into high drifts – even the front door blew open and there was a snowdrift in the hallway! This was great fun for the children of course, but hard work for the adults. The animals still had to be fed and milked, dairy work had to be done and milk delivered – all this when the air line for the milking machines used to freeze up and water in the draughty dairy didn't come through. Washing and filling milk bottles was one of the coldest jobs imaginable and later, on the round, the milk in the bottles froze and pushed the lids off. However, it meant there was no risk of the milk going sour! The van was left at the top of the drive so's not to get stuck and was loaded up with milk by tractor. Some days Derek Lay, one of the farm workers, took milk crates on the tractor to strategic points around the village. From there, Ruth and Keith and sometimes the children used sledges to haul the crates around the lanes to the houses."

'The floods of 1968 were bad for us. In the yard was an Austin J4 van, which was a high one, but the water covered the whole of the engine. It was almost unbelievable. There must have been a big collection of water higher up and all of a sudden it came down.'

"On 16 July '68 summer storms caused a swell of water coming down from the hills, across Home field, which had been recently ploughed, crashing through the fences and sending torrents of muddy water across the yard, outbuildings and into the house. The water washed pigs out of the barn window – they went swimming down the Combe. Keith, Ruth and 'Granny' Statham tried carrying stuff upstairs to stop it getting spoiled. Eventually there was about 3 to 4 feet of water all through the downstairs rooms in the farmhouse. Also the electricity went out. Gradually, during the night, the water subsided leaving a layer of mud and stubble everywhere. Again, the family was unable to claim against any insurance as floods are considered an act of God."

"During five decades Ruth and Keith delivered milk to around 400 houses in and around Blagdon, Burrington, Rickford and Upper Langford never missing a day. In the early days there was a delivery every day, including Sundays, but later they delivered double the amount on Saturdays so that Sunday could be a day of 'rest' – time to sort out the bookwork, making up bills, putting up cream, as well as cooking a Sunday lunch and getting off to chapel!"

A typical summer's day

A typical day began at 4am when the cows were turned out on to Burrington Ham; it was light at that time in the summer. At 6:30am they were brought in for milking by two cowmen – for a long time these were Jim Lay and his son Derek. After milking, they were turned out on to the Blackdown side of the road. 'At one time, they used to turn out the cattle on the Ham in the afternoon, but that wouldn't do because of all the people about.' The cows were brought back across the road for afternoon milking around 4pm, after which they were put in 12-acre field as there was no water for them on the Blackdown side of the road.

"*Ruth's round was the early morning one – leaving the farm at 5:00am – there was nothing to beat seeing the early morning mist rising over the lake, being the first to walk on newly fallen snow, hearing the dawn chorus start up, seeing night creatures such as foxes, owls, rabbits, hedgehogs, deer, in the quiet morning. However, the deliveries weren't always early as Keith would often get a thousand and one other chores done around the farm before he went out.*"

Ruth would often cover Burrington and Upper Langford before joining up with the main round. She always took pen and paper with her so she could jot down ideas which came into her head – she had always enjoyed writing poems from an early age and has published three books to date with one in the pipeline.

Bill Lye was a coalman; he always said that the milkman worked harder than the coalman. Bill would say, 'They're in and out of every house every day; I only go once a fortnight.' Keith agreed it was jolly hard work. 'If you went out on a Sunday walk, you were thinking – I must get back for Sunday afternoon milking.' John reminded Keith that he was known in the village as the 'midnight milkman': 'They didn't know if you were delivering that night's milk or tomorrow morning's!'

"*Wet and windy days were no fun, neither were Mondays when all the extra milk bottles were returned, involving extra journeys back to the farm. Then there were car break-downs and other technical hitches! There were various houses on the round where Ruth and Keith were well looked after with welcome cups of tea! The Lye family at Pen Cw offered a scrumptious Christmas dinner for the family to enjoy to save cooking on the busiest day of the year. The Misses Edwards along Street End always used to leave Mintoes sweets with the money each week and many other customers would leave gifts during the festive season in appreciation of Ruth and Keith's unfaltering service.*"

Fig. 14 – Five-gallon churn and small can used to carry milk for domestic use

Fig. 15 –
Ten-gallon milk churn
with bottom of milking unit
(lid and cowclusters missing)

Milk Containers

Fig. 16 - Lower Ellick Farm in 1918, the 18-gallon churn was used on the railway. Keith is a baby in his mother's arms, the cattle are Shorthorns. The man in the foreground was the photographer, the picture was taken with a delayed shutter.

Fig. 17 – Guernsey/South Devon cattle

Keith was often exhausted on his rounds, walking into hedges and even, one night, driving into the bank while coming up the Combe. Sybil Avery's family was worried one night when he passed their cottage in Street End Lane and did not return. They went out to find him fast asleep at the wheel. 'That's in the past now, we have had 10 or 11 years of real rest.' After retiring, Keith still got up at the same time and took their dog on to the Ham – many a time he has been stopped by police! 'It was terrific hard work; thank goodness none of the family have gone into farm work. It is even worse now, it's all wrong, all the land round the hills is up for rent now – who wants it?'

Farm machinery and livestock

The Weavers still have the old hand-operated cream separator and the later electric model, both of which were used on the farm. The electric model is made of stainless steel and is as good as ever it was. Electricity came to their farm long before the Watts at Rhodyate Farm on Two Trees; the supply probably followed the houses up Ellick Road. Before electricity, separators were geared up for hand operation and acted as centrifuges where cream comes out on one side and skimmed milk on the other. Today different grades of milk are obtained by taking off different 'cuts' (fig. 14, 15).

'Our cream was always a bit thicker and a good colour, coming from Channel Island cattle, it was close to today's extra thick double cream.'

They never produced clotted cream on their farm, because it was a lot more trouble. Surprisingly, Keith does not take milk in his tea today, but he does like cream on his breakfast cereal!

Their first tractor was an Allis Chalmers 'Row-crop' – Keith's father used to refer to it as 'Alice'. Then they had a Fordson followed by a David Brown. Before the tractor, about three horses were kept along with the pony, which was mother's wedding present. 'In the early days, father used to take milk to Burrington Station for transport to Bristol and the pony was always a devil to catch.'

Ernest started with Dairy Shorthorns (fig. 16) but changed fairly soon to Guernseys after the occasion when they had 17 Shorthorns react to the TB test. They sold the Shorthorns to Evan Osmond, a dealer who arranged to send in Guernseys from Gloucester Market.

'They gave better milk. We carried on like that for some time before one had brucellosis. Then we never bought in any more and bred our own.'

When they found that the Guernsey calves were not fetching anything like the price of beef cattle, Jack Struggles, one of the AI men, recommended crossing with South Devon. Their milk still commanded a premium price and the calves were worth more. They were nice animals, lighter in colour than pure Guernseys, but with a heavier coat (fig. 17).

A working life of 60 years comes to an end

By the early 1990s the rules regarding the selling of green top (untreated) milk became more bureaucratic and the red tape surrounding it just produced one hassle after another. When Keith had to pay for a dead cow to be taken away, it was the last straw. At the age of 74 Keith decided to retire and Unigate bought the round. Their live and dead stock was sold and they remained on the farm for a short period before moving to their present home in the nearby village of Lower Langford.

Fig. 18 – Keith and Ruth Weaver at home June 2007
(author's photograph)

"In recognition of Ruth and Keith's long service record, a group of villagers organised a fantastic tea party for them at Coombe Lodge, to which the whole village were invited. Many contributed cakes etc and about 300 people were present. Terry Lyons ran a free bus. This was a truly memorable afternoon – the warmth of well-wishers, gifts, presentations, speeches, as well as an ensemble playing music throughout the afternoon. Ruth and Keith were presented with a large basket of flowers, a poem written and illustrated by villagers, a pair of binoculars and a cheque for over £1,200."

The poem was very cleverly constructed and *"of course there was a reply poem by Ruth."*

We all will miss our Mendip milk
for it will come no more

Energy giving, wholesome & fresh
delivered to each door

Always it was brought to us
through sun, rain, wind & sleet

Velvet cream we'd ordered too
for special Sunday treat

Even more than pintas
we'll miss the Weavers' care

Regard they had for neighbours old
for them found time to spare

Stories told to youngsters shy
of wild-life round the farm

May Ruth & Keith now take a rest
and lead a life more calm

Indeed we wish you gold-topped
years may you walk peaceful ways

Large crates of thanks we offer you
a milkchurn full of praise

Know also bottles full of love
are yours for all your days.

Sources

The two primary sources for text in this article were:

1.   Keith's meeting with the Recent History Group

Keith Weaver met with members of the Recent History Group on 6th March 2003 in Court Lodge. Mike Adams (MA, scribe), John Gallop (JG, chairman), Sybil Gallop (SG), Anne King (AK) and Daphne Watts (DW) were present. All contributed to the session which was recorded. In this article, **'single quotes'** surround what Keith said, unless another speaker is specifically mentioned.

At subsequent meetings of the group, corrections and amendments were made and items of interest were added, which related to the original discussion. More drafts followed and Keith and Ruth made their comments. Factual details have been checked as far as possible but this article is not claimed to be anything other than the collective memory of those who took part in the meeting. That said, it hopefully adds to our understanding of life in Blagdon in days past.

2.   The Weaver Family History – a private family album.

This album is a short history of the family and the milk round days compiled for Ruth and Keith by their children. In this article, extracts are shown in **"double quotes."**

Illustrations

John Chamberlain	Fig. 2b
Weavers family album	Figs. 2a, 3, 4, 5, 6, 9, 10, 11, 12, 13, 16
Keith's 80th birthday album	Fig. 7, 17
Author at Weavers' home 11/6/07	Figs. 1, 8, 14, 15, 18

Notes

1   The land is regulated by the Conservators of Burrington Commons.
2   These flowers were lost when the land was ploughed up during the Second World War. Yellow rattle still grows today in at least one field in the neighbourhood, which appears to be managed in the traditional way.
3   Today the bracken is harvested to make organic compost which is sold in selected local outlets. The composting is done at Middle Ellick Farm.
4   The school took pupils from age 5 to age 14, which was the regular leaving age.
5   This is an extract from 'The Weaver Family History' denoted by "double quotes."
6   An article on the railway by the same author appeared in Volume 2 of 'A History of Blagdon.'
7   Keith began driving in 1935 at the age of 17. Fred Lye also drove on the rounds.
8   A tape of Ruth's reminiscences has been produced.
9   Expanded by Ruth 20th June 2007.
10 Subsequently renamed Greengate (singular).
11 The author visited Keith and Ruth at home in Lower Langford to finalise the text and take photographs – on Monday 11th June 2007 with their younger daughter Elaine and on Monday 18th June with their elder daughter Alison.

Some Blagdon Houses visited by the Somerset Vernacular Building Research Group (SVBRG)

Tony Beresford

Introduction *(Neil Bentham)*

In January 2005 I contacted John Dallimore, a founding member of the SVBRG, to ask if the Group would be prepared to venture over the border into the district of North Somerset[1] and in particular the village of Blagdon on the north side of the Mendip Hills, to help us with the dating of some of our older village houses. John kindly agreed and the outcome of the Group's work is the subject of this short essay.

By way of an introduction to the origins and work of the SVBRG the following information is based upon the pamphlet they publish for anyone needing their expertise. The Group was established in 1979 with the remit to record and study the traditional houses and buildings of the historic county of Somerset, in particular the farmhouses, cottages, smaller manor houses and barns which were built in the local style and out of the local materials.

The group has a membership of some 75 people from all walks of life who are united in their interest and passion to study and understand the underlying reasons for the creation of a wide range of building types which have survived for centuries and still continue to meet the needs of an essentially rural population.

Houses and other buildings are recorded by a team of four or five people who, depending on the size and complexity of the property, might spend from a few hours to the better part of a day on the task. The team welcome a preliminary escorted tour of the building, where the owner can point out features of interest that may not always be obvious. Roof spaces and cellars are of particular interest, since they often contain original features that have survived in the dark of a roof space or the damp gloom of a cellar and been undisturbed for centuries. In addition to the careful recording and measurement of the internal features a similar detailed survey of the external features is recorded.

Since 1996, several dendrochronology (tree ring dating) projects have been undertaken, which has enabled the establishment of the chronology of the seven principle roof types found in Somerset as well as the dating of various styles of beam mouldings. Michael Worthington of the Oxford University Dendrochronology Laboratory has assisted in one of the Blagdon houses.

The Group's final report will contain scale drawings and an interpretation of how and when the house or building developed. The study is solely concerned with the architectural features and history of the building and makes no reference at all to the current usage of rooms, the location of modern features or details of movable objects. A copy of the report is given to the owner and, with his or her consent, a copy is deposited in the Somerset Record Office at Taunton and the National Monuments Record Centre at Swindon.

Although no fee is charged for the services of the SVBRG a donation towards travelling and other costs is appreciated and to this end a portion of the BLHS Heritage Lottery Fund grant enabled the surveys of some eight Blagdon houses to be undertaken during 2006 and 2007.

The BLHS records its thanks to the owners of the houses listed below for their kind permission and co-operation in allowing the members of the SVBRG to Survey their houses:

property	location	period	owner(s)
Blagdon House	Station Road	C16, C17, C18	Jonathon and Susan Hoey
Walnut Tree House	Garston Lane	C17, C18, C19, C20	John and Naomi Lyons
Park House	Park Lane	early C18	Paul and Diana Brunning
Court Farm House	Station Road	C16, C17, C19, C20	Roland Eagling
Hannah More House	Church Street	C17, C18, C20	Lawrence and Katie Davies
(John Chamberlain provided additional information to the team.)			
Gilcombe House	Church Street	C16, C17, C18	Andrew Barnes
The New Inn	Park Lane	late C16 and C17	Roger and Jackie Owen
The Old Saddlery	Park Lane	late C17 and early C18	Alistair and Kirstie Mann

It should be noted that there are other old houses in Blagdon that have yet to be surveyed but these will have to await further funding becoming available in the future. In addition, the following houses were given a cursory look, without any survey notes, but sufficient to give an opinion as to dating:

property	location	period	owner(s)
Pound Corner	Garston Lane	late C16, C20	Peter and Jenny George
Stones Cottage	Station Road	Early C16, C20, C21	Jane and John Venner-Pack
Kings Cottage	Station Road	Early C16, C20, C21	Dick Wood
Fir Tree Farm	High Street	late C15, C17,C19,C20	Mell and Roger Kaye

(Fir Tree Farm was initially surveyed by Pam Brimacombe, Ron Gilson and Vince Russett)

The BLHS also thanks the members of the Group, in particular John Dallimore, for their time and expertise in helping us to obtain some reliable data about those houses that have survived thus far into the 21st century:

The SVBRG members who surveyed the Blagdon Houses were:

Tony Beresford – Chairman
John Dallimore (Projects Co-ordinator)   John Clarke
Vera Headlam   Barry Lane
Pam Paget-Tomlinson   John Rickard
Denny Robbins   Angie Roberton
Susan Shaw   Carolyn Young

Dr Peter Hardy, geologist, has provided additional expertise in identifying stone features in two of the houses, and Michael Worthington has advised on the potential tree ring dating possibilities in one of the houses.

The following reports are summaries of the more detailed surveys but it is intended that the results will provide the answer to our question, 'when was this house built?' From that information it should be possible to begin to understand how the village developed over the centuries.

Tony Beresford, Chairman of the SVBRG, wrote the summaries which are reproduced below. Full copies of the surveys are available for perusal in the BLHS archive.

❧   ❧   ❧   ❧   ❧

Gilcombe House, Church Street

This rubble stone house comprises a two-storey main range with two one-and-a-half storey lean-to additions at the rear and a single storey addition to one side.

The front two rooms to the left of the current hallway date from the 16th century, the entry being through what is now a door in the hall. At this time only the first room was heated, the other being an unheated service room. The house had an upper floor from the outset and would then have been one-and-a-half storey.

In the early- to mid-17th century the house was upgraded with a room added at the south end. This room has an elaborate framed ceiling of four main panels, divided by smaller beams into a total of sixteen panels. The fireplace in this room has an elaborate moulded bressumer, which is replicated in a slightly smaller version in the room above. For reasons that are unclear the front wall is not aligned with the original building.

The whole house was upgraded in the 18th century. New stairs were inserted, the upper floor was rearranged and the eaves and roof raised, with new larger windows inserted on both floors. The service rooms on the far left hand side of the house were probably added at this time as a kitchen, perhaps a bakery, and separate access to the servant quarters.

Hannah More House, Church Street

This rubble stone house is roughly square in plan and originally was one-and-a-half storey (that is the upper floors were partly within the roof space). The main door was placed centrally at the front of the house. There were two main rooms, a hall to the left of the doorway and a kitchen to the right. At the rear of the kitchen was a service room and behind the hall a possible parlour. The wall thicknesses, details of the beams and the remaining original roof timbers indicate that the house was probably built in the early 17th century, although the window in the service room behind the kitchen may be a remnant of a slightly earlier building

During the mid-20th century the house was altered. The roof was raised and new first-floor windows inserted. The central doorway was blocked and the principal entry moved to its current position, effectively in the fireplace of the original hall.

Walnut Tree House, Garston Lane

The main and original part of this rubble stone house is of two full storeys, with later single storey additions at each end. It originally had two ground floor rooms, a smaller living room entered directly from the street and an unusually large service room. The stair is of solid baulk construction and its position rising from the original living room is uncommon, but known from a few other examples in Somerset. (Usually the stair would be alongside the fireplace.) The details of walls, beams and the partition suggest a date in the 17th century, although the baulk construction of the stairs is more usually found in earlier houses.

The north extension was probably a stable built in the 18th century. In the 19th century, the house was divided into two and further alterations and additions made at that time.

New Inn, Park Lane

This building seems to have been developed over the 17th and 18th centuries, progressively moving up the hill. It is not clear what the function of each addition was and there is some evidence of the re-use of some windows and roof trusses from elsewhere.

The earliest part was (and still is) one-and-a-half storey and was probably a simple single ground floor room dwelling dating from the early 17th century. It had a winding stair beside the fireplace. The next part appears to have been built as two full storeys from the outset, with two ground-floor rooms, one each side of the present doorway. Although much altered, this appears to have been added in the mid- to late-17th century. The final part was built as a two-storey single-room cottage, probably dating from the 18th century, and was shown on the 1886 Ordnance Survey map as a separate dwelling.

Park House, Park Lane

The present two-storey house is a complex amalgam of part of a late-medieval house and, at a lower level, an early 18th century house with a mid-19th century lean-to at the rear and an early 20th century lean-to to the left (southern side).

Details of the fireplace and framed ceiling in one room at the rear of the south end indicate that this was probably the hall of a good quality late 15th century house of which nothing else remains. If correct, then the rest of this house would have been aligned east-west parallel to the contour, whereas the current house is aligned north-south.

In the early 18th century a two storey two-unit, central-entry house was added at a lower level to the remnant of the earlier building. The room to the left of the doorway was probably a parlour and that to the right a kitchen. A tie-beam roof covers the whole building including the late-medieval part. The date 1705 inscribed on the front is likely to be correct for this part of the building.

The lean-to extensions on the west side were added as service rooms in the mid-19th century when access to the oven, which would have originally been from the kitchen fireplace, was reversed. A further lean-to at the south end was probably built in the early 20th century.

The Old Saddlery, Park Lane

Built of rubble stone, the house has an almost square plan of double-pile form (that is, it has two parallel roofs with the ground floor divided by a central wall). It is one-and-a-half storey throughout and was probably thatched. The house appears to have been built in two stages and the narrower rear range is an addition to the original small two room house. The door opened directly into the living room and a partition to its right divided off a smaller inner service room.

The thickness of the west wall and the slightly wider west range suggests that it was built in the late 17th or early 18th century. The roofs over the front and rear ranges are very similar, so the rear range was built soon after, possibly in the mid-18th century to replace a lean-to extension.

The date stone of 1727 on the south-west chimney stack cannot be *in situ* as the original building was unheated at that end. It may have been relocated when the house was enlarged.

Court Farmhouse, Station Road

The house, of rubble stone, is now of two full storeys with four rooms in line together with a staircase turret and a part-storied rear wing.

The original house, the two rooms to the right of the present doorway, was one-and-a-half storey comprising a hall and inner room with two chambers over. The common-rafter roof, which survives underneath the present roof, and the details of the framed ceiling in the hall and other features indicate an early 16th century date. The plan form of this part of the building, including a central rear stair turret, has been found elsewhere in north Somerset. The two rooms to the left of the doorway, approximately the same size as the 16th century house, were added in the mid-17th century. A large kitchen wing, including a curing chamber beside the fireplace, was added late in the century, probably to provide extra service for the northern addition. The house is no longer a farm and the farm buildings have been converted into housing.

Blagdon House, Station Road

Fundamentally a full two-storey 18th century house, with fielded panelling in the parlour to the left of the main doorway and in the chamber over, and a fine central well staircase extending the full height from the ground floor to the attic, this house has earlier origins.

The cellar under the parlour would seem, from the evidence of a heavy ceiling beam and a window at the head of the cellar stairs, to be the remnant of a 16th century house. (The cellar is reported to be the only one in Blagdon.) The kitchen wing at the right-hand rear of the house, with a possible curing chamber to the left of the fireplace and an oven to the right, might be the remnant of a 17th century building.

A dendrochronology report on the cellar beam is awaited.

[1] The District Council of North Somerset was established, under the Re-organisation of Local Government Act, on 1st April 1996. It replaced a part of the former County of Avon, which was established by an earlier re-organisation of local government on 1st April 1974. It was the 1974 re-organisation that brought to an end, with much local opposition, the original County of Somerset that had been in existence for over 1300 years, since about 658, following the battle of Peonnan, as described in *A History of Somerset* by Dr R.W. Dunning (Somerset County Council Library Service, 2nd edition 1987).

Appendix A

LECTURE TOPICS, OPEN FORUM MEETINGS AND EVENTS HELD AND PLANNED FOR 2007

Jan. 18th	World Wars I and II★	
Feb. 15th	Traditional Songs and Music of Bristol	John Shaw
Feb. 16th	Trilith Association of Old Films (Joint meeting with Harptree History group)	Olga Shotton
Mar. 15th	My Life on a Mendip Farm★	Mary Smith
April 19th	A Look at BLHS Photo Archive □	Sheila Johnson
May 17th	Bristol Water and the Mendips★	Paul Hodge
June 21st	Bristol Conned (Famous Deceptions)	William Evans
July 19th	Visit to St Andrew's Parish Church★	John Chamberlain & Dick Wood
Aug. 9th	Launch of *Blagdon and Mendip voices* CD	Tony Staveacre
Sept. 20th	The Work of the Wheelwright	Mike Horler
Oct. 18th	Household Appliances and Services★	
Nov. 15th	Mendip Lodge & the Rev. Dr Thomas Whalley	Prof. Chris Stephens
Dec. 14th	Launch of Volume 3	

Programmed Events

February	Launch of Volume 4

★   *C20 Village forum event*
□   *The new data projector was used*

Appendix B

The topics listed below are awaiting the interest of willing researchers. Those marked ★ are being actively researched.

> Blagdon School★
> Bristol Waterworks and Drainage
> The Cemetery
> Old Coombe Lodge★
> Blagdon deeds★
> Blagdon wills
> Church embroidery★
> Electrical, Gas, Telephone and Postal Services
> Fire Services
> The geology of the local area
> Aspects of family history
> Field names
> Food, cider and orchards
> The Home Guard★
> Lords of the Manor
> National Service★
> The Normans and Domesday
> Turnpikes and Transport
> Blagdon and the New Poor Law 1834★
> Population growth and occupations in Blagdon★
> Police Services
> Sports and pastimes
> St Andrew's church – part two★
> Newspapers and the Press
> The Charterhouse Murder★
> Churchwardens' Accounts★
> Vestry minutes★
> Dame Janet Stancomb-Wills★
> WW2 and Blagdon ★

The Society would be pleased to receive articles, photographs, and memorabilia from the community and, in particular, offers to undertake the basic research on any of the topics listed above – or any other topic that helps to illuminate *The History of Blagdon*.